The Little Book Of
HEROIN

Robert Ashton
Sanctuary

CONTENTS

INTRODUCTION

The world is in the grip of a frightening drug: heroin. Crime, poverty, dependency, death and destruction trail in its wake. Over a century's experience of fighting the drug has failed to kill or tame it and heroin's stranglehold remains as tight in the 21st century as it was in the 20th. The drug has been outlawed for most of its life and abused almost since the day it was discovered in the late 19th century.

In every western country its use has grown considerably in the past few decades and the production of opium, the raw material used to manufacture heroin, has increased exponentially to meet demand. There's no question, heroin is here to stay.

...and it presents a massive problem. Heroin is made dangerous because it is traded by criminals and almost always misused. It is illegally supplied, cut with myriad - and sometimes noxious - adulterants, and often used in harmful and unhygienic environments, causing problems for both user, society and governments. The latter, picking up the bill for everything from soaring crime rates to spiralling healthcare costs.

The challenge facing the world's governments is how to deal with it. For most of its life, more and more prohibitive laws have been introduced to deal with heroin. But, as Prohibition in 1920s and 1930s America demonstrated, a total ban has largely served to entrench global drug cartels and create billions in funds for the criminal organizations that run them.

Society's obligations to provide education about heroin, prevent life-threatening temptation and treat chronic addiction became more sophisticated in the second half of the last century, with methadone programmes and advertising campaigns. Any successes have rarely been clear-cut, however, because heroin spins a complex web of issues and problems, and the pace of change around its orbit often outstripped the legislators and doctors; the moral climate shifted, new research revealed new problems, heroin supply increased, heroin prices dropped and purity levels improved.

This means that methods and tools for tackling the problem need to be continually adapted and reviewed. That's the difficult part – changing minds and policies that deal with heroin always poses tricky trade-offs and judgements about their impact, essentially because it is the young who are most at risk.

But, by the 1990s, that radical sea change had begun to take place. A more enlightened, better-managed and better-financed approach to the problem was adopted by several countries. Some European governments and a number of other western-model countries, notably Australia, began to take harm-reduction issues more seriously. Treatment, not punishment, became the new watchword.

The speed of this change was clearly demonstrated by the UK's experience. In 1998 its first 'drugs tsar', Keith Hellawell, unveiled a ten-year drugs strategy based around young people, communities, treatment and availability, setting major long-term targets: to cut heroin use by 25 per cent in 2003 and, by 2008, halve its use, reduce its availability by 50 per cent and double the number of heroin abusers in treatment.

By 2001 some of these targets were believed to be unachievable; Hellawell's role as anti-drugs co-ordinator had been sidelined; and, although his strategy template was still being applied, it was under review. It appeared that the problem of heroin was beginning to be seen more as a public health issue than a criminal one.

In 2002 UK police chiefs broke new ground by recommending that heroin users be sent for treatment rather than prosecuted, and the reintroduction of widespread prescription of heroin was being examined by a Home Affairs Select Committee and the UK's National Treatment Agency.

Further, a former UK cabinet minister and a serving police chief added their voices to the pro-legalization of heroin lobby, which seeks to break the drug's link with crime and to hand governments a sizeable income from taxing its legal sale. It is argued that these funds, potentially worth millions, can then be used for addiction treatment or prevention.

However, after more than a century of living with heroin and its associated problems, it is clear that there are no easy solutions. Complete prohibition hasn't worked, yet legalization of heroin or even decriminalization remain distant, and bring with them their own problems of control and increased demand.

As countries, their governments and their populations become more mature and sophisticated with regard to their perceptions of the drug and its use, politicians and experts will continue to weigh the evidence for an overhaul of drug laws, and examine and test new techniques for dealing with heroin. In the meantime, the drug's hold remains firm.

CULTURE

HEROIN IS HEADLINE NEWS

The impact of drugs on modern media and culture has been enormous. Arguably, though, heroin has had more success than any other at imprinting its bewitching power on to the cultural consciousness. The media is fascinated by heroin. The public fear it. And politicians make capital from it.

As the 20th century turned into the 21st, there was no let-up. In fact, heroin was filling increased acres of newsprint and giving anxious leader writers more opportunities to warn of the drug's perils.

In 1997, for example, when the leafy Texas town of Plano was haunted by a string of heroin overdoses, the drug was rarely off the front page of US tabloids and the leader position in radio broadcasts.

In Britain another banner headline, 'This Is How Heroin Killed Our Girl', in March 2002, reminded everyone that the drug doesn't discriminate. Beneath the headline were two pictures of the same girl, Rachel Whitear. One showed her dressed in her school uniform; the other was a harrowing colour shot of Rachel dead. The 21-year-old university dropout had been found on her knees, slumped on the floor of a bedsit, a hypodermic syringe still clasped in her hand. She had been dead three days.

The 11 September terrorist attacks on New York also had the effect of reinforcing heroin's media profile as the ultimate evil. US President George W Bush didn't hesitate to link heroin with the 21st century's first big battle: the war against terror. The drug was perceived as an ally of Osama bin Laden's al-Qaeda terrorists and the Taliban regime, which ruled Afghanistan until its overthrow in late 2001.

HEROIN CHIC

Although ubiquitous, heroin's success has been bolstered by its ability to reinvent itself and add new layers to its myth. This was most notable in the early 1990s. Before then, it was perceived by most as a drug for losers – Wall Street winners used cocaine.

Images of junkie losers with dirty needles in filthy squats were replaced with scenes of bone thin, sexy models in filthy squats. Heroin wasn't just dangerous, it was cool. And once it made it on to glossy double-page fashion spreads it soon passed from the underground to the mainstream. Wall Street brokers traded their coke spoons for smack spikes.

Dubbed 'heroin chic', photographers like Corinne Day, David Sims and Juergen Teller shot fashion spreads against seedy backdrops with models who appeared strung out, their dark-rimmed, sunken eyes reflecting an elegantly wasted look.

The dangers of a heroin epidemic being unleashed were recognized by former US President Bill Clinton when he attacked the fashion industry for popularizing heroin chic in May 1997. He said, 'They [fashion leaders] are admitting flat out that images projected in fashion shoots in the last few years have made heroin addiction seem glamorous and sexy and cool. And as some of those people in those images start to die now, it has become obvious that that is not true. You do not need to glamorize addiction to sell clothes.'

But the fact that the rich and the famous were using heroin gave editors the opportunity – and excuse – to fill their pages with pouting photographs of models and actors, which compounded the link between heroin and fame. Heroin had acquired a new image, far from dirty needles and hookers in dark alleys.

Heroin use has escalated and its cultural influence is more prevalent than it has ever been. It's possible to put together a whole heroin-themed jukebox, starting out by slipping Alice In Chains' 'Junkhead' or The Velvet Underground's 'Heroin' out of the CD collection.

Even the local cinema could mount a smack retrospective, kicking off with the double bill *Requiem For A Dream* followed by *French Connection II*. And for a heroin read, library shelves are literally groaning under the weight of all the literature – Irvine Welsh's *Trainspotting*, Luke Davies' *Candy* or practically anything from William Burroughs – celebrating the drug.

HEROIN MOVIES

A 1997 study of movie rentals in the USA found that 22 per cent of the 200 most popular films depicted illicit drugs and about a quarter of those (26 per cent) contained graphic portrayals of their preparation and use. Also, surprisingly, very few (15 per cent) contained an anti-drug message.

In the very early years of cinema, drug use and the possession of narcotics were not legislated upon and an opium user or heroin addict didn't carry the moral stigma they do today. This meant a crop of US and European movies set in opium dens – such the 1906 French film *Rèves D'Un Fumeur D'Opium* ('The Opium Smoker's Dreams') – played in theatres before legislation and changing social attitudes dictated a new agenda in Hollywood.

The first attempt to curb the proliferation of heroin and morphine in film came in October 1927. In an attempt to stave off rigorous censorship, the Motion Picture Association agreed to endorse and boycott a list of 36 controversial subjects drawn up by Will Hays. The use of drugs and drug trafficking were listed near the top of this list. This was reinforced by the 1930 Motion Picture Production Code, which prohibited any mention of addiction or trafficking on screen. This gave the Production Code Administration

(PCA) a licence to deny a seal of approval to any film that broke the code, effectively dooming its release.

For the next two decades sex not drugs occupied the moral guardians. Then, in 1955, Otto Preminger's *The Man With The Golden Arm* blasted apart the taboo surrounding narcotics abuse, with Frank Sinatra portraying heroin addict jazz drummer, Frankie Machine. The film was in violation of the PCA, which refused to grant it a certificate; however Preminger released the film himself. Its success helped convince the PCA to amend its code a year later to allow treatments of drug addiction. Although the audience never gets to see the needle in Sinatra's arm he is seen preparing to tie off a tourniquet and the camera lingers on his face as the rush hits. Heroin had become a major movie star.

Since the early 1970s, smack movies have been packing them in. In 1970 Paul Morrissey's *Trash* featured the first shot of needle puncturing skin. But it was 1971 that was to herald a turning point for the drug: in that year no fewer than four mainstream heroin movies were screened. *Jennifer On My Mind* was released alongside *Born To Win* (aka *Addict*), starring George Segal, T*he Panic In Needle Park*, which made Al Pacino's reputation as an actor, and Floyd Mutrux's *Dusty And Sweets McGee*. The latter featured a character getting a fix under his tongue and, like many early heroin movies, did not stack the screen with authority figures expressing their moral outrage about the drug.

The 1980s saw a shift of emphasis to concentrate on real-life casualties: Sid Vicious, Charlie Parker and Chet Baker were all featured in biopics. In 1989, Gus Van Sant established the cinematic vocabulary and visual template of the contemporary heroin movie with *Drugstore Cowboy*.

Film-makers began to realise that an injection of smack into a movie script will always fill seats. Visually, what gives heroin the drop on other drugs is that it isn't simply snorted, smoked or swallowed. There is the whole shocking paraphernalia of the junkie: the syringes, the belts for tying off, the cotton wool and spoon are all perfect props for the cinematographer to shoot in close-up. The act of injecting is much more visually shocking than popping an E. The syringe will break skin and then fill with blood as it hits a vein. It'll also leave the film's character with lasting physical effects and they will wear these track marks and scabs like battle scars as the movie draws to its climax.

Moreover, heroin wasn't just appearing in films. Real-life Hollywood stars had come to embrace the drug. River Phoenix, who played a junkie hustler in Van Sant's *My Own Private Idaho*, died in 1993, aged 23. Blood tests verified the presence in the actor's blood of alcohol, Valium, heroin, and cocaine, the last two being the vital ingredients of a speedball.

A few years later, Robert Downey Jr, an Oscar nominee, fought a public battle against heroin and other drug addictions, culminating in rehab and a prison sentence on the back of narcotic and weapons charges.

HEROIN MUSIC

It's an old story. Heroin and music. Since the turn of the last century musicians have enjoyed an uneasy – and often devastating – association with heroin. It has spawned songs, even movements. Progressive rock was an unfortunate side effect of LSD; the nihilism of punk's blank generation and grunge ran on heroin.

Musicians have been singing about it or dying from it since Charlie Parker, Miles Davis, Art Pepper, and Chet Baker defined 'cool' in the 1950s. They used heroin to ease the days between the long sweaty nights blowing their horns or mashing the piano keys. Then heroin was cool. In his frank memoir about heroin, *The Trumpet And The Spike*, Baker admits that most of the musicians he played with were on junk and that 'spiking myself became a gesture as automatic as lighting a cigarette is with you'.

The British mod scene in the early 1960s fuelled itself on purple hearts, and the hippies saw out that decade by opening their minds with LSD and magic mushrooms. But of course, heroin never really went away. Iggy Pop, Keith Richards, and Lou Reed were all users. But their influence on lifestyle didn't spread much beyond New York's East Village or those who bought The Velvet Underground's *White Light/White Heat*.

Punk's arrival in 1976 was ostensibly about blowing away anything that had gone before. Two drugs it didn't dispense with were speed and heroin. Johnny Rotten was scornful of heroin and – for the most part – the British punks at the Roxy contented themselves with amphetamines. His fellow Sex Pistol Sid Vicious was to become dope's heroin ambassador. Vicious was soon a smack casualty. Out on bail on a charge of stabbing his junkie girlfriend Nancy Spungen at the Chelsea Hotel, Sid died of an accidental overdose in New York.

However, by the early 1990s heroin wasn't playing second fiddle to any other drugs. It was *the* drug. In the USA, street heroin was becoming increasingly pure, although the price remained resolutely stable. Snorting and smoking became popular. Seattle was gaining a reputation as the heroin capital of America and one of the city's bands, Nirvana, were providing the bleak soundtrack for a new youth movement: grunge. Heroin was the drug to play when they dropped the needle on *Nevermind*. Suddenly every band had a junkie, detoxing, getting busted, or passing out in photo shoots.

HEROIN-RELATED DEATHS IN ROCK

- In 1959 Billie Holiday finally succumbed to the twin ravages of heart disease and heroin under police arrest on a hospital bed.
- Frankie Lymon's career came to an abrupt stop in 1968 when the singing sensation (he was the frontman in Frankie Lymon And The Teenagers) was discovered on the bathroom floor of a New York apartment with a syringe by his side.

- In 1970 the hit of the Monterey Pop Festival, Janis Joplin, died of an accidental heroin overdose in the bedroom of her suite at the Hollywood Landmark Hotel. At 27, she was at the peak of her short career.
- Jimi Hendrix died of a barbiturate overdose within weeks of Joplin, but the 27-year-old guitarist had been a known user of heroin.
- Aged 27, Jim Morrison was found dead of heart failure in the bath at his Paris apartment in 1971. The full facts surrounding the premature death of The Doors' vocalist in the early hours of the morning are still unclear, although it is thought he acquired a fix earlier that night and, if that didn't cause the fatal heart attack, many blame his death on the cumulative effects of his heavy drug use.
- The 24-year-old Scottish drummer of The Average White Band, Robbie McIntosh, was killed at a Hollywood party in 1974 after he was spiked with a lethal dose of heroin.
- Tim Buckley died in his sleep in 1975 after snorting prodigious amounts of heroin supplied by a friend.
- Just months after his girlfriend Nancy Spungen was found stabbed to death in New York's Chelsea Hotel, punk rocker Sid Vicious scored a lethal dose of heroin and suffered a fatal overdose in his sleep. He was 21.
- Darby Crash of the Los Angeles punk band The Germs died of an overdose at the end of 1980, just a week after reforming the group.

- After years of heroin addiction and a career that remained resolutely underrated, singer/songwriter Tim Hardin died at the end of 1980.
- Malcolm Owen of UK punk group The Ruts, who dealt with his heroin addiction in many of the band's lyrics, lost his battle with the drug in 1980.
- Heroin split The Pretenders, literally. Guitarist James Honeyman-Scott and bass player Pete Farndon both met their ends after taking speedballs in 1982 and 1983 respectively.
- Red Hot Chili Peppers lost their 26-year-old lead guitarist when Hillel Slovak's drug lifestyle caught up with him and he died of an overdose in 1988.
- Chet Baker was hooked most of his adult life. Before his death in 1988 – falling from a hotel room in Amsterdam – the drug ravaged his film-idol looks, drew him beatings from connections, earned him dozens of busts on narcotic violations, and landed him a spell in Riker's Island jail.
- After more than a decade of heavy drug abuse, the former New York Dolls, and Heartbreakers, guitarist Johnny Thunders died of a heroin overdose in New Orleans in 1991. The proto-punk, who was 38 at the time of his death, recorded The Ramones' classic 'Chinese Rocks' and often played it at gigs.
- In 1994, Nirvana's Kurt Cobain was found dead. The guitarist/vocalist with the Seattle-based grunge band,

had struggled with years of smack abuse. Although Cobain shot himself, he delivered the self-inflicted fatal injury just a week after almost succumbing to a heroin overdose.

- Kristen Pfaff, the 27-year-old bassist in Courtney Love's female grunge band Hole, died of an overdose in a bathroom in 1994.
- The drug-related lifestyle of Grateful Dead's Jerry Garcia finally caught up with him in 1995 when he died from health complications during withdrawal from heroin addiction.
- While preparing for a Blind Melon concert in New Orleans in 1995, the group's 23-year-old singer, Shannon Hoon, died of an overdose.
- Jonathan Melvoin, keyboardist with Smashing Pumpkins, died of an overdose in a Manhattan hotel in 1996.
- In 2002, Alice In Chains' lead singer Layne Staley was found dead in his Seattle home. Staley's long-time battle with drug dependency was a central component of the band's sound, which included the song 'Junkhead'.

HEROIN LITERATURE

Books about smack are a writer's dream. All that hollow-cheeked desperation and grubby hopelessness sends authors scurrying to their word processors, clutching their thesauruses tightly. Junkie lit offers opportunities for some unremittingly bleak prose, dark, dark characters – everyone

loves a loser and you can't get a better loser than a junkie
– and a dramatic final chapter in which someone overdoses
in a grubby council flat.

As a plot device, heroin can take off in any direction the
author wants to go – from introspective angst, as in Alexander
Trocchi's *Cain's Book*, to crazy road odyssey in *Go Now* by
Richard Hell. The rituals connected with heroin use, from
the cooking to the injecting, are excellent vehicles to show
off literary dexterity. The vocabulary for jacking up can easily
up a writer's word count if the plot is running out of steam,
and those similes and adjectives just can't be reined in when
it comes to writing about veins, needles and blood.

THOMAS DE QUINCEY

There's no doubt that heroin has inspired a wealth of ground-
breaking and searing work, all the more so when written
by an author with first-hand experience of addiction. This
applies to one of the earliest memoirs on the subject,
*Thomas De Quincey's Confessions Of An English Opium
Eater*, published in 1822.

This autobiographical account of his opium addiction is
De Quincey's most famous work. The writer took opium to
ease physical pain but became addicted to it. The book charts
the psychological effects of the drug, from the euphoria of
his initial experiences to the darkness and nightmares arising
from long-term usage. Richly written, it is a seminal tale of
the effects of addiction on a brilliant mind.

COLLINS, KIPLING, AND CROWLEY

In the days when books about drug addiction were frowned
upon, it was a very daring author who would break the
taboo and shine a light on such behaviour. In Wilkie Collins'
1868 novel *The Moonstone*, opium is used as a plot device
for both its medicinal properties and its exotic and deviant
connotations.

Rudyard Kipling's 1901 novel *Kim* also makes a pointed
comment about the ready availability of opium in India, and
its power to addict and corrupt.

In 1922 Aleister Crowley shocked British Victorian
society with his book *Diary Of A Drug Fiend*. Crowley called
himself Beast 666, totally rejected the Victorian hypocrisy
of his day and was a constant user of heroin, cocaine, opium,
hash and peyote. *Diary Of A Drug Fiend* was an eye-opener
to those who knew little of drugs, but Crowley wanted to
show the true nature of drug addiction, that there were
moments of joy and elation, not just despair.

WILLIAM S BURROUGHS

Burroughs is the classic junkie lit author who lived it, and
Junky is generally regarded as a classic of its type. *Junky*
starkly recounts Burroughs' decades-long addiction to
heroin. Written when the USA was in the grip of anti-drug
hysteria, the first edition contained a number of disclaimers
by the publisher whenever Burroughs made some
unorthodox claims about the nature of addiction. The

disclaimers were outlined at the beginning: 'For the protection of the reader, we have inserted occasional parenthetical notes to indicate where the author clearly departs from accepted medical fact or makes unsubstantiated statements in an effort to justify his actions.'

ALEXANDER TROCCHI

Yet there are others who believe the contrary, that heroin destroys brains and creativity. In 1960, *Cain's Book* by cult Scottish writer Alexander Trocchi was published. Known as the 'Scottish Beat', Trocchi was a heroin addict who turned his young wife to prostitution to pay for drugs.

JIM CARROLL

In 1978 the role of author who lived it was passed on to the poet, playwright, musician and author Jim Carroll whose memoirs, *The Basketball Diaries*, were based on his own heroin addiction. The book covers the period 1962–6 when the teenage Carroll, growing up on the mean streets of New York. He tells of his posh private schooling and his years playing basketball, stealing and hustling gay men to support his growing heroin addiction.

In the 1980s heroin seemed to have been overtaken by other drugs as a literary muse. Writers like Brett Easton Ellis and Jay McInerney favoured cocaine and tranquillizers as plot drivers, and bright young things snorting Charlie from toilet seats occupied young fashionable novelists. Heroin all but disappeared from the bookshelves and it wasn't until the 1990s that it made a comeback – in spectacular fashion.

The protagonists of books like Linda Yablonsky's semi-autobiographical novel *The Story Of Junk* and Peter Trachtenberg's memoir *7 Tattoos* are swamped by the mechanics of drug use, which the authors clearly find more fascinating than characterization and plot.

It probably took the work of Will Self in the 1990s and Irvine Welsh's *Trainspotting* to revitalize the genre. Self, journalist and writer, first injected heroin at 17 and was a full-time junkie for almost 20 years. Many of his short stories and articles deal with heroin and addiction, but he is strongest when writing about the drug as an incidental element within a story.

Welsh could never be accused of taking his subject too seriously and although he doesn't stint on the despair of addiction, he manages to wring a lot of humour from his subject. The protagonists have no future, but Welsh doesn't moralize.

The appeal of heroin to this latest generation of writers goes beyond its illegal status. Heroin doesn't give up. It has a definite hold on a writer like no other drug – especially a writer who is an ex-user. Luke Davies is a poet and writer whose novel *Candy* didn't follow the usual drug novel path. It's a love story first and a heroin novel second and, although the presence of heroin is powerful and all-pervading, the relationship between two people and the nature of obsession is the central theme.

HEROIN STREET SLANG

Heroin's long history, cultural impact and prevalence among literary figures – with a poetic bent for adding to the argot – has ensured that it probably has more slang words associated with it than any other drug.

There are hundreds of different names for heroin. The death of John Belushi in 1982 gave some heroin users the inspiration for another name to describe the speedball cocktail of heroin and cocaine, which led to the comic's demise. And, following the death of River Phoenix in 1993, some culturally aware addicts in north Hollywood and Santa Monica would, for as long as the actor's name continued to appear in newspapers, talk about 'falling' or 'swimming in the river' when they jacked up. Bart Simpson, the character from the TV show *The Simpsons*, has also been added to the slang list, as has TV host Jerry Springer.

With the drug's capacity to suddenly end life neither is it any coincidence that, more than any other drug, the slang draws on words associated with death ('heaven dust', 'dead on arrival', 'hell dust') or its methods ('bombs away').

There is a definite geographical bias to the slang, which operates at a countrywide or even citywide level. Thus, 'chieva' or 'black tar', a type of cheap heroin smuggled up from Mexico, and which has flooded west coast US cities, is popular around Haight-Ashbury in San Francisco, but will never be used in the estates around Moss Side in Manchester, where 'skag' has entered the vernacular. However, a London junkie in a Brixton squat may often prefer to use the more widespread 'smack'.

Even illegal drugs have brand names and heroin is no exception. In New York and many other US cities, dealers often branded the heroin they were supplying, even accompanying this with a distinctive logo on the $10 (£7) bags it was sold in. Some well-known 'brands' include names that are designed to appeal to the target consumer group by drumming home the dangerous outlaw status of the product: Homicide, Poison, Kill City, Last Payday, Body Bag, Lethal Injection, Silver Bullet.

By picking ever more outrageous names the dealers demonstrated they had learned a lesson from the media and advertising: shock sells and an established brand can lead to customer loyalty. These brands were traditionally sold from one spot and were recognizable because they would consistently have similar levels of purity and be cut with the same – non-narcotic – additives. In short, the addict knew what they were getting.

02 HISTORY

POPPY'S PROGRESS

Heroin is made from morphine, a naturally occurring substance found in the seed of the opium poppy. The history of heroin, therefore, starts with the opium. And this begins with the cultivation of the poppy, *Papaver somniferum*. The milky fluid extracted from the plant's ovary is highly narcotic after drying. This is opium, the name derived from the Greek word for 'juice of a plant'.

Around 3400 BC the first poppy was cultivated in lower Mesopotamia. Some archaeologists also claim to have found evidence of fossilized poppy seeds, which suggests that Neanderthal man may have used opium over 30,000 years ago. Excavations of the remains of Neolithic settlements in Switzerland have unearthed evidence that the poppy may have been cultivated then: perhaps for the food value in the poppy seeds.

The first reference to the poppy appears in a Sumerian text, which refers to it as Hul Gil, the 'joy plant', and the Sumerians soon passed on the art of poppy culling – and its euphoric effects – to the Assyrians. Some 2,000 years

31

later, the Babylonians introduced opium to the Egyptians, who began to cultivate fields around Thebes.

Priests encouraged the use of opium preparations for remedies, sometimes called thedacium after the potent Thebes poppy fields. A trade in opium soon flourished, throughout the reigns of Thutmose IV, Akhenaton and King Tutankhamen, with the Minoans and Phoenicians operating profitable routes across the Mediterranean into Greece and Europe. It also became common practice to entomb pharaohs with opium artefacts.

In 460 BC the father of medicine, Hippocrates, acknowledged opium's use as a narcotic and styptic in treating internal diseases and, by AD 400, Alexander the Great had introduced opium to Persia and India, and Arabic traders were shipping the poppy to China.

Opium became a taboo subject during the Inquisition and it largely disappeared in Europe during the 14th and 15th centuries. However, by around 1500 the Portuguese had discovered that smoked opium produced instantaneous effects, and smoking the narcotic began to be the accepted method of taking the drug.

In 1527 opium was reintroduced into Europe through laudanum, a mix of alcohol and the drug, which was discovered by the Swiss physician Bombastus von Hohenheim. This gave successive generations, who added various spices to produce their own versions, access to mass sedation.

By the mid-17th century, opium had become the main commodity of British trade with China, its use thus taking root in the Far East. By 1839 it had also caused a war between the British and Chinese. The East India Company had enjoyed a monopoly on shipping opium from Bengal into China, and had ridden roughshod over Chinese licences imposed to restrict imports of the drug by selling it to Indian merchants who smuggled it for them.

Despite the instigation of a House of Commons Committee of Enquiry in 1830, set up to investigate the company's opium dealings, the £2 million ($2.9 million) trade continued unabated, causing an epidemic of addicts among the Chinese population. At its highest point it was believed that there were around 15 million opium users.

In 1839 the Chinese government finally acted and confiscated some 20,000 chests of opium from British warehouses in Canton. In 1840 the British Foreign Secretary, Lord Palmerston, sent out a force of 16 British warships, which besieged Guangzhou and threatened communications with the capital.

This first Opium War was settled in 1841 with the Treaty of Nanking and China ceding Hong Kong to the British. The opium trade with China continued, with new trading partners – the French and Americans – becoming involved in shipping the drug.

Some 15 years later Britain and China fought a second war when, in 1856, Chinese officials boarded and searched a British-flagged ship, the *Arrow*. The French joined the British in launching a military attack in 1857, at the end of which they demanded that the Chinese agree to the Treaty of Tianjin in 1858. This opened further ports to western trade and provided freedom of travel to European merchants inland. Trade in opium nearly doubled over the following two decades, but by this time China had also begun to grow its own poppy, which it traded in over the next century.

Many literary figures were also being seduced by opium, including John Keats, Shelley, Byron and Thomas De Quincey, who, in 1821, published his autobiographical account of opium addiction, *Confessions Of An English Opium Eater*. And, in 1860, the English doctor Thomas Sydenham was moved to write, 'Among the remedies which it has pleased Almighty God to give to man to relieve his sufferings, none is so universal and so efficacious as opium.'

Opium is a complex chemical cocktail including sugars, proteins, fats, gums, ammonia and myriad alkaloids, notably morphine, codeine, noscapine, papaverine and thebaine. Apart from thebaine, these alkaloids are used as analgesics and can reduce or abolish pain without loss of consciousness. However, it wasn't until 1805 that German scientist Friedrich Wilhelm Sertürner isolated the first alkaloid in its pure form from opium. Sertürner named the substance morphium (morphine) after Morpheus, the Greek god of dreams and sleep. It wasn't until a decade later that the powerful effects of morphine – the drug had at least ten times the potency of opium – were recognized and in 1821 a London pharmacist began producing it. Six years later German manufacturers E Merck & Company began the commercial production of morphine and in 1836 morphine entered the London Pharmacopoeia.

A new technique for administering the drug – and a crucial tool for today's junkie – arrived in 1843 when an Edinburgh-based physician, Dr Alexander Wood, discovered the process of injection using a syringe. Injected morphine is up to 300 per cent more potent and, because the effect is almost instantaneous, it rapidly led to the intravenous use of the drug as a painkiller and for recreational use.

Opiate abuse in Europe and the USA had increased significantly by the mid-1800s. Opium dens, often run by Chinese immigrants, were opening in most American cities and even in Old West towns where cowboys sat out herding duties laid up in dimly lit rooms smoking opium with prostitutes.

Opiate consumption in the USA also received a boost following the American Civil War in 1866. The wounded had been treated with morphine intravenously on the battlefield and, consequently, tens of thousands of soldiers became addicts. The medical establishment began to raise concerns about a new epidemic: morphine was being used by European and American doctors as a remedy to combat opium dependency and the addict would simply switch his addiction to morphine. Also, many patent medicines around at this time, such as laudanum and paregoric, contained opium extract. By the end of the 1890s the United States was desperate to curb the non-medical use of opium.

Then a new drug was discovered, diacetylmorphine, or heroin. It was first synthesized from morphine by the English researcher CR Alder Wright in 1874, by boiling morphine with acetic anhydride over a stove. He was trying to isolate a powerful but non-addictive alternative to morphine. He failed. The white crystalline powder he discovered is between three and eight times more potent than morphine...and easily as addictive.

However, this wasn't realised at the time. In 1895 Heinrich Dreser, who was in charge of drug development at German drug manufacturers Bayer, began production of diacetylmorphine and coined the name 'heroin' after the German word for hero, *heroisch*.

Dreser tested the new synthetic drug on animals, human volunteers and himself, and declared it was an effective treatment for a range of respiratory ailments, including tuberculosis, asthma, coughs, emphysema, and bronchitis. He also declared that the drug was not habit-forming. In 1898, *The Lancet* introduced it to British physicians. It advised, 'Heroin is said to be free from other disagreeable secondary effects of morphine.'

Commercial production of heroin began in 1898 and it was advertised by Bayer as a sedative for coughs rather than an analgesic. It was prescribed for a wider range of respiratory problems, such as whooping cough and hay fever. Doctors were also assured that its effects on motor skills and intellect were minimal.

Some dissenting voices warned of the dangers of addiction but, despite this, free samples of heroin were handed out to physicians. They often treated their patients' complaints with small doses of heroin administered orally via pills or pastilles, and drug companies manufactured over-the-counter drug kits containing a glass-barrelled hypodermic needle and vials of heroin. Bayer was soon selling heroin to dozens of countries, including the USA. The sales pitch was that it was a cure for morphine addiction: the modern heroin addict was born.

However, by the early 1900s doctors began to notice that patients were consuming inordinate amounts of heroin-based cough remedies, and that heroin addiction in the UK and USA was out of control. Users – and the medical profession – soon realised that an addiction to heroin was more problematic than an addiction to morphine.

Heroin addiction in the USA became linked to legislative measures directed against illegal drugs and recreational usage, such as the introduction of the Smoking Opium Exclusion Act 1909, which meant that American opium smokers found it difficult to find affordable opium. They switched almost exclusively to heroin, with heroin snorting soon becoming the popular method of administration.

During World War I, politicians and the media also whipped up a climate of hysteria against dope fiends enslaved by heroin. However, the arrival of the Harrison Act only managed to spread heroin use. Before 1914 most drug users remained loyal to one narcotic, but when new laws meant that their supplies of cocaine and other drugs were cut, they turned instead to cheap heroin. And once they had tried heroin, they stuck with it.

Heroin was finally outlawed in the USA in 1924. By that time, though, the market was already well established. There were too many addicts – some estimates put the figure at 200,000 by the mid-1920s – for the health authorities to deal with. These addicts had already found ways to pay for their drugs and support their habit. They were turning to crime, principally stealing scrap or junk metal. Consequently, they became known as junkies – the name stuck.

HEROIN MANUFACTURING, PURITY AND TYPE

Heroin is a semi-synthetic opiate produced from morphine. But its journey to New York's East Village or London's Soho starts as the milky sap of the opium poppy – Papaver somniferum – probably grown in a field somewhere in Afghanistan, Pakistan or Myanmar.

Growers often use a technique called slash-and-burn farming to prepare the poppy fields for planting. After all the trees have been cut down and the vegetation has been cleared and burned, the farmers sow the poppy seeds.

Poppies can take about three months to mature, but harvesting will take place at different times of year depending on the part of the world they are being grown in. Just before reaching maturity, the poppy plant produces a flower, which indicates it is ready for harvest. After about a week, the flower petals fall off, leaving a capsule.

Raw opium gum is harvested from this capsule. The surface of the capsule is cut or scored with a knife containing three or four small blades and the opium gum oozes out. The following day, the gum is scraped off the capsules with a flat tool. Each capsule is usually scored in this manner three to five times, or until no more gum exudes out.

After the harvesting process is complete, the capsules are cut from the stem, allowed to dry, and broken open so that the seeds inside the capsule can be used for next year's crop. Once the gum is collected, the farmer sets it out to dry for several days and then wraps it in plastic, or sometimes banana leaf if it has been harvested in Asia. Opium gum is dried, washed, boiled and reboiled to form the gumlike opium, which is ready for smoking. This also has a very long shelf life and can gain value over time.

Opium is used as a substitute for modern medicines in some remote areas, such as Southeast Asia, because few medical supplies are available. There are dozens of alkaloids in opium, but the principal ones of interest to recreational drug users are codeine and morphine. Codeine is often used in cough medicine or mild painkillers, but is not nearly as powerful as morphine and will usually only be of interest to drug abusers if their regular supply is cut.

Morphine is up to 1,000 per cent stronger than opium and is used medically as an analgesic in its pharmaceutical form, as a suppository, pill or an injectable ampoule. Often the supply found on the streets is from medical stock following a burglary at a pharmacy and legally produced morphine pills are also smuggled from countries such as India.

Refining raw opium into heroin is a long, multi-step process. The opium gum is transported to a refinery and converted into morphine, which is dried and made into bricks ready for the chemical process to convert them into heroin. The morphine and acetic anhydride, used in the manufacture of film and synthetics, are then heated together at temperatures of 85°C (185°F) for six hours, which forms impure diacetylmorphine (heroin).

Water and chloroform are added to precipitate impurities before draining and the addition of sodium carbonate to solidify the heroin. Activated charcoal is used to filter the heroin out of the sodium carbonate solution and then it is purified with alcohol before being heated to evaporate off the alcohol.

PURITY

The refining process has been perfected to the point where heroin purity levels above 90 per cent can be achieved by the time the product leaves the refinery. Heroin's appearance can vary quite considerably depending on the manufacturing process and how much it is refined. Pure heroin is a white, odourless powder with a bitter taste.

However, because most heroin is illegally manufactured, levels of purity and colour can vary considerably depending on the production process involved and the sub-stances with which the drug has been cut in order to maximize bulk and profit. The commonest non-narcotic adulterants include baking powder, chalk, glucose powder, caffeine, quinine, flour, talcum powder, powdered milk or sugar. The colour can, therefore, vary dramatically from dark brown, through beige to pink and white.

Pure heroin is rarely sold on the street. A bag – slang for a single dosage – may contain 100mg of powder, but only a fraction of that will be heroin; the remainder could be anything. In the 1970s the purity of heroin in a bag ranged from 1 to 10 per cent. However, in the mid-1990s drug enforcement agencies found that it was ranging between 15 and 99 per cent, and was routinely 50 per cent or more pure.

This was because dealers on the street, realising that higher levels of purity meant users could inhale or smoke the drug without the fear of HIV associated with intravenous needles, attempted to expand their market beyond the injecting junkies. The higher levels of purity also reflected the greater amounts of heroin available. In 2000, the US national average of heroin purity was 35 per cent, and in the UK in 2002 it was running at around 47 per cent across a purity range of 2 to 90 per cent.

Analysis of the US Drug Enforcement Administration (DEA) drug buys and seizures between 1981 and 1997 shows that purity increased from 7 per cent in 1981 for purchases of 0.5g or less, to 36 per cent in 1988 and rising to 56 per cent in 1997.

TYPE

Crude morphine is sometimes called heroin number one and the white to off-white, pale grey or dark brown, powdered or solid heroin base, prior to its conversion to hydrochloric salt, is called heroin number two. A hard granular material, light brown, dark grey, red or pink in colour, and containing between 25 and 45 per cent heroin hydrochloride and cut with other (sometimes non-narcotic) substances, is called heroin number three. This is also a smokable form of the drug.

The most highly refined heroin, with a purity level of 98 per cent heroin hydrochloride, no additives and white in colour, is heroin number four. Similarly, the medium-brown hard chunks of crude heroin produced without a purification process and between 40 and 60 per cent pure with a vinegary odour, are often referred to as 'brown heroin'.

One of the most crudely processed types of heroin is black tar, which is illicitly manufactured in Mexico and has become popular in the USA in recent years. This has a purity level of between 30 and 60 per cent heroin hydrochloride, is very dark brown or black coloured, and either sticky like roofing tar or hard and brittle like coal. Again there is a strong vinegary smell and it appears to melt when heated.

SYNTHETIC DRUGS

Heroin is manufactured, but its roots are clearly from the opium poppy. However, many other drugs exhibit similar effects but don't rely on the poppy for their source material. These are called synthetics and are mostly produced legally for medical use, but are illegally traded on the streets.

Many users of these clinical opioids, which often have recognizable brand names, believe they are safer than heroin simply because they are manufactured in licensed laboratories. Sometimes, however, these 'designer drugs' are produced in illegal laboratories and are often more dangerous and potent than heroin if misused.

FENTANYL
Known on the street as 'china white' and one of the most commonly known opioid analogues, fentanyl was introduced in 1968 by a Belgian pharmaceutical company as a synthetic narcotic to be used as an analgesic in surgical procedures because of its minimal effects on the heart. Fentanyl is particularly dangerous because it is 50 times more potent than heroin and can stop respiration rapidly, although the euphoria is less than morphine. This is not a problem during surgical procedures because machines are used to help patients breathe; however, on-the-street users have been found dead with the needle used to inject the drug still in their arms.

DEXTROMORAMIDE
An opioid analgesic used for the treatment of severe pain. It is short-acting and causes less sedation than morphine. Dextromoramide is available in tablet form or as a suppository and may cause depression of breathing.

ACETAMINOPHEN-OXYCODONE

This is a combination of two different types of pain medicine used to treat moderate to severe pain. Generic acetaminophen-oxycodone tablets and capsules are available, but the powerful painkiller is only available on prescription and normally dispensed only to the terminally ill. Oxycodone, known as 'percs' on the street, has been dubbed 'hillbilly heroin' and has been responsible for hundreds of deaths in the USA. Essentially a synthetic form of morphine, the tablets are crushed together to provide a hit, and experts say it is more potent and more addictive than heroin. The small white tablets can be swallowed whole, crushed and snorted or mixed with water and injected. Each tablet costs £5-20 ($7-30) depending on its strength.

PETHIDINE

Pethidine is an analgesic and an anti-spasmodic, which is a drug that helps people relax. It's a similar drug to morphine, which midwives often prescribe and administer during childbirth. It is given as an injection and often combined with another drug – an anti-emetic – to control sickness. For drug abusers it can produce a short buzz.

DIHYDROCODEINE

The opioid dihydrocodeine (DHC) is frequently used as an analgesic and is one of the most commonly prescribed painkillers in the UK, but can cause severe constipation.

BUPRENORPHINE

Buprenorphine is available by prescription (under the brand name Subutex) as a treatment for heroin. It has been found to be effective in preventing the need to use heroin and also in helping people to withdraw. But buprenorphine, which is also prescribed to treat severe pain, became a real problem in the 1980s when it was used illegally as a heroin substitute on the streets.

PENTAZOCINE

The effort to find an effective analgesic that is less dependence-producing led to the development of pentazocine. Introduced as an analgesic in 1967, it has frequently been encountered in the illicit trade, usually in combination with tripelennamine. It can give users morphine-like effects if the tablets are dissolved and injected; some users have also reported that it can cause hallucinations.

DIPIPANONE

Dipipanone hydrochloride is medically used as a painkiller and can be taken orally or injected after it has been crushed and dissolved in warm water. It is a very strong painkiller (often prescribed to cancer patients) with definite physical dependent-forming potential, as it causes strong withdrawal symptoms and signs similar to heroin and morphine use. However, the high silicon content of the drug means that veins can quickly silt up, causing circulation problems.

METHADONE

Synthetic methadone was devised by German chemists during World War II at the German group IG Farbenindustrie. Also called 'dollies' by abusers, methadone works well taken orally and can be effective for over 20 hours. Prescribed as a substitute for heroin, it comes in several different formats: tablets, 10mg ampoules, a linctus, and a liquid green, yellow or brown mixture, which usually contains glucose and chloroform water to dissuade injectors.

HEROIN COCKTAILS

Drug users don't usually confine their choice of narcotic to just one. Heroin dependants are no different. Most are poly-drug or multiple-substance abusers.

Some heroin addicts use a multitude of different narcotics, but alcohol, tranquillizers, barbiturates, amphetamines and cocaine are the most popular. The junkie will use them when their regular supply of dope is cut or their dealer is out of town, to heighten the effect of heroin and, sometimes, to help them cope during withdrawal.

Mixing heroin with other drugs can have two effects: it can increase the buzz and the danger. Pairing dope with barbiturates, tranquillizers or alcohol can cause severe depression of the central nervous system and lead to coma and death.

Also, the combination of heroin and alcohol often causes vomiting, which is particularly dangerous if the mix of the drugs has caused unconsciousness. Cocaine and heroin are the best-known double act: the speedball. The ultimate stimulant paired with the number one soporific.

HEROIN PRODUCTION

The global supply of illicit opium, the raw material for heroin, has varied enormously in the last century. But the real growth in supply – to meet the demand for the drug – kicked off in the 1980s when production levels tripled from around 1,000 tonnes/tons in 1981 to 3,000 tonnes/tons less than a decade later.

By the 1990s production levels hit the 5,000 tonne mark and remained relatively stable until 2000, although a bumper Afghan harvest of 4,600 tonnes/tons in 1999 helped boost worldwide production to 5,800 tonnes/tons. Despite this increase in production, the global area under opium poppy cultivation in 1999 was almost 20 per cent less than in 1990, when over 250,000ha (617,500 acres) was under cultivation. This suggests that cultivation techniques had improved over the decade and producers were able to gain better yields per hectare.

In terms of the global heroin market, Afghanistan and Myanmar (formerly Burma) are in a league of their own. They are by far the biggest producers of opium, accounting for over 90 per cent of the opium produced in 2000. Figures for 1999 suggest that Afghanistan alone had a total area under cultivation of 91,583ha (226,210 acres) and, by the late 1990s, Afghanistan was estimated to be the source of 75 per cent of the world's heroin and 90 per cent of the supply that found its way to the UK.

With such a monopoly on the global market, natural disasters such as droughts, improving law enforcement, a new government regime and - in the case of Afghanistan - a war, could have a massive effect on the world's supply.

AFGHANISTAN

Opium has flourished in Afghanistan's southern desert region and northern provinces since the time of Alexander the Great. The poppies are well suited to the rugged terrain and arid climate, requiring little water or attention, and making them easier and cheaper to cultivate than wheat and other crops.

The poppy crop and trade in heroin has thrived through countless regimes, from the 1933-73 reign of King Zahir Shah, through the Soviet occupation during the 1980s, the bloody years of the Mojahedin and the rise of the fundamentalist Taliban in the 1990s.

The Taliban surprised illegal producers and traffickers in 2000 when the government's leader, Mullah Mohammed Omar, issued an edict outlawing opium production in Afghanistan. As the world's largest producer of heroin throughout the 1990s, the Taliban, which had seized control of the country in 1996, had earned millions from the heroin trade because drug traffickers were required to pay the

Taliban's commerce ministry a 10 per cent tax on cultivation profits and 20 per cent on smuggling profits.

Afghan farmers were forced to turn to planting other, less profitable, crops or vineyards in place of their poppy fields and only areas under the control of the opposition Northern Alliance continued to produce opium. The result was that poppy cultivation fell to just 7,706ha (19,034 acres) in 2001 from 82,515ha (203,812 acres) the year before.

Some experts believed the Taliban may have been attempting to strangle supply and drive up the price of opium on the international market. This would have had the effect of significantly increasing the cost of a bag of heroin on a New York or London street. The economics supported this theory: in September 2001, when there was no prospect of a fresh crop under the Taliban, 1kg (2¼lb) of opium cost between $570 (£390) and $655 (£450).

The 11 September 2001 attacks on the twin towers of New York's World Trade Center changed that. The USA traced the terrorists' network to Osama bin Laden's al-Qaeda network, which was being harboured by the Taliban in Afghanistan. The war against terrorism that followed, and the subsequent fall of the Taliban regime at the end of 2001, meant the Afghan farmers reverted to their more lucrative crop: opium. The motivation wasn't hard to find. In the 1990s the opium trade was estimated to be worth around $98 million (£68 million) to Afghan growers and a farmer, fresh from the crippling conflict with the defeated Taliban, could have expected to make thousands trading with Pakistani and Iranian buyers if he replanted his wheatfields with opium at the end of 2001.

One radical solution proposed was for European governments to buy the poppy crop, but this would have been highly controversial as well as costly. There was also recognition that providing aid and substitute crops to poor farmers would not necessarily solve the problem because any attempt to control the trade would be resisted by local warlords.

EU External Affairs Commissioner Chris Patten blamed Afghan-sourced heroin for 'devastating' lives and funding organized crime. He added, 'Beating drugs helps beat terrorism and will help Afghans have a brighter future.'

MYANMAR

Myanmar, formerly Burma, is part of Southeast Asia's infamous 'Golden Triangle', which also comprises parts of Laos and Thailand. It is also the world's second largest producer of illicit opium and in 1999 had 89,500ha (221,000 acres) under cultivation.

Illegal drugs have had a long history of supply and manufacture in the country, although it was only in the last decade of the 20th century that Myanmar became a global capital for opium growing and heroin production, helping to fuel the number of addicts worldwide.

The manufacture and supply of heroin in the country boomed following the bloody takeover of the country by the Law and Order Restoration Council (renamed the State Peace And Development Council [SPDC] in November 1997) in 1988. Drug lords, who had close links with Burma's army dictators, were able to act almost with impunity, and there was a lack of commitment from the government towards stamping out narcotic trafficking and the money laundering that followed it.

There were some successes, such as the surrender of drug warlord Khun Sa. He was the leader of the southern Shan state and on America's 'Most Wanted' list following an indictment on narcotics racketeering charges in a New York court. But some commentators argued that his arrest was largely a public relations exercise and that the government was practically a trade partner in the cultivation, supply and manufacture of illicit drugs.

This was largely confirmed when a ceasefire was called in the late 1990s. This essentially gave the opposition parties free rein, leading to massive increases in the opium harvest and purer forms of heroin on the street. Between 1988 and 1997 the average purity of heroin shot up from 34 per cent to 62.5 per cent. The US State Department stated in its 2000 International Narcotics Control Strategy Report: '...the ceasefire agreements have permitted former insurgents to continue their involvement in narcotics cultivation and trafficking activities.'

OTHER MAJOR HEROIN PRODUCERS

After Afghanistan and Myanmar, the Lao PDR, Colombia and Mexico produced the largest quantities of illegal opium in 1999. They had 22,550ha (55,700 acres), 7,500ha (18,500 acres) and 3,600ha (8,900 acres) of poppies under cultivation, respectively.

Opium production in Mexico and Latin and Central American countries such as Peru and Venezuela, was mainly destined for the US heroin market at the beginning of 2002, with Colombia replacing Southeast Asia as a prime source of the drug in the late 1990s: 65 per cent of the heroin seized in the USA during this period was sourced from Colombia.

Other major opium producers in 2002 included Pakistan, Thailand and Vietnam. However, production of opium and heroin fell in Southeast Asia in the late 1990s, and Thailand and Pakistan also drastically cut cultivation, with the latter reducing the number of hectares under the poppy from 7,500ha (18,500 acres) in 1990 to just 3,000ha (7,400 acres) in 1999.

China, the largest producer of opium in the inter-war period, Guatemala in Central America, Lebanon, Iran and Egypt, which all had fairly sizeable fields under cultivation, had also reduced production to practically zero by 2000.

HEROIN SUPPLY AND TRAFFICKING ROUTES

Once the opium crop has been harvested, raw opium or heroin is trafficked across the globe to the main drug centres. Sometimes this can involve long and complex routes, facilitating the use of every imaginable mode of transport – from donkey to aircraft.

Trafficking of heroin and the main routes via which it is shipped can be traced by the number and pattern of seizures. Generally seizures of illicit drugs have increased, with 170 countries around the world reporting drug seizures in 1997/98 compared to 120 in 1980/81.

However, heroin is not the world's most widely trafficked drug. Of those countries that successfully seized drugs in 1997/98, only 91 per cent reported finding opiate substances, including heroin, compared with 98 per cent of the countries that reported finding cannabis products in their hauls.

However, along with the increase in the number of countries reporting seizures, heroin trafficking has shown an upward trend over the last 30 years. Less than five tonnes/tons of the drug was seized each year between 1975 and 1980, but by 1998 this had increased to nearly 35 tonnes/tons.

Of seizures of heroin and morphine in 1987/88, 72 per cent were made in Asia, with some 42 per cent discovered in Iran, reflecting its proximity to the trade routes coming out of Afghanistan. As befits its status as the world's largest opium producer, Afghanistan is the main supplier of heroin to a wide range of countries, from neighbours such as Iran and Pakistan to western European markets, including France and the UK.

The UN warned in early 2002 that unless measures were successful to stop the harvest of that year's Afghan opium crop, then the 'best ever opportunity' to suffocate the illegal trade would be lost. The Taliban ban on poppy growing in Afghanistan, introduced in July 2000 and coupled with severe droughts in 2001, reduced Afghanistan's opium yield by 91 per cent in 2001. It was thought, however, to have had little effect on trafficking throughout Europe because traders had stockpiled significant amounts of heroin along their supply routes.

Between 1987 and 1988 Europe accounted for about 23 per cent of worldwide seizures, at over 10,000kg (22,000lb), with most taking place in western countries including Turkey. The Americas accounted for about 3.7 per cent of heroin and morphine seizures in 1997/98.

In 1999, over seven tonnes/tons of heroin were seized in the EU, of which one-third was accountable to the United Kingdom. Heroin seized in the EU comes mainly from the so-called 'Golden Crescent' – a mountainous area including Iran, Afghanistan and Pakistan – followed by the 'Golden Triangle' routed via Turkey, the Balkans and The Netherlands. However, after 2000 smugglers moved their routes north and US drug enforcement agencies reported that the number of heroin shipments from Afghanistan through the central Asian states to Russia had increased; Tajikistan was a favourite destination. In 2002 one heroin trade expert estimated that only 20–30 per cent of heroin was shipped to Europe via the usual Iranian-Turkish route.

At EU level, heroin seizures increased up until 1991/92 and then stabilized. The number of heroin seizures has grown steadily in Luxembourg, Portugal and Sweden since 1985, while marked decreases have been reported since 1996/97 in Austria, Belgium, Denmark, France, Germany and Spain. In every member state, the quantities seized fluctuated over the period. In 1999, marked decreases in the quantities of heroin seized were reported in Austria, France, Greece, Ireland and The Netherlands, while in Italy and Spain there were large increases in the amount of heroin seized.

Seizures in the UK increased by more than 80 per cent in 1999, which is significant because the UK already accounted for around 30 per cent of all heroin and morphine seizures in the EU during 1997/98, more than The Netherlands (about 20 per cent) and Germany (12 per cent). In 2001 it was reported that Afghanistan and the Golden Crescent were the source of 90 per cent of the heroin reaching Britain's streets.

The impact of the drug trade from Myanmar has been felt by its neighbours, Bangladesh, China, India, Singapore, and Thailand. They all experienced increased incidents of heroin seizures, a rapidly expanding community of addicts and a rise in HIV in the 1990s. In a 1998 survey throughout the northern state of Kachin, over 90 per cent of heroin users tested HIV positive.

Turkey has always been an important part of the heroin map and, between 1990/91 and 1997/98, heroin and morphine seizures in the country have increased by more than 10 per cent to over 3,000kg (6,600lb). In the late 1990s Turkey, midway between the producer countries Afghanistan and Pakistan and the European market, also emerged as a final destination and transit territory for acetic anhydride, one of heroin's major precursor chemicals, which is manufactured throughout Europe and shipped to Asia.

The majority of heroin crossing Turkey is shipped along the Balkan route to its final destination, although some new developing markets emerged in eastern Europe in the late 1990s and many countries along the main trafficking routes – such as Iran, Pakistan and Central Asian countries – became bigger buyers.

Pakistan, which shares a border with Afghanistan, remains an important player in the global heroin market despite a decline in seizures during the 1990s because of a reduction in domestic production and large scale re-routing of heroin traffic via Iran. However, Pakistan still accounted for 9 per cent of all worldwide heroin and morphine seizures in 1997/98 and its geographical importance was demonstrated in 1999 when large amounts of Afghanistans's bumper opium poppy harvest of 4,600 tonnes/tons were shipped across the country, leading to an increase in seizures.

India, the world's largest legal opium producer, has improved controls over manufacturing and cut seizures of heroin and morphine by more than 60 per cent between 1990/91 and 1997/98, with seizures in 1997/98 between 1,000kg and 3,000kg (2,200lb and 6,600lb).

Around 16 per cent of global seizures in 1997/98 were made in Southeast Asia, an area incorporating the notorious Golden Triangle, traditionally one of the main outlets for heroin. However, there were some radical changes in trafficking patterns in the 1990s with Thailand's importance as a main route in the area diminishing. By 1997/98 Thailand only accounted for around 5 per cent of all seizures of opiates in Southeast Asia, compared to almost 60 per cent in the late 1980s.

The Asia-based criminal networks supplying the USA have virtually been squeezed out of the market, although there is evidence that Southeast Asian heroin is being smuggled into the United States in smaller multigram or multikilogram amounts by couriers or mail and package delivery services.

Its place in the league of suppliers has been taken by China, where heroin was smuggled directly from Myanmar for export to the USA, usually via Hong Kong. However, poor weather conditions in 1999 reduced production, and seizures in China were down 30 per cent that year.

The US heroin market is supplied entirely from foreign sources of opium produced in four distinct geographical areas: South America, Mexico, Southeast Asia and Southwest Asia. In 2000, 1,415kg (3,119lb) of heroin was seized in the USA under the Federal-wide Drug Seizure System, which includes the DEA, FBI and US Customs. This was significantly up on the 1,239kg (2,732lb) seized in the previous year.

Trafficking patterns have changed significantly since the mid-1990s when Southeast Asia was the main supplier for the North American markets and accounted for around 3 per cent of global heroin and morphine seizures in 1997/98. By 1999, however, Southeast Asia accounted for only around 10 per cent of heroin seized in the USA, and Southeast Asia accounted for just 6 per cent.

The flow of South American heroin began to increase dramatically around 1993 when Colombia-based gangs, already in control of the cocaine trade, expanded into heroin. They quickly saturated the USA heroin markets using Dominican distribution rings and by providing low-cost, high-purity heroin. They also employed surefire marketing tactics such as providing free samples of heroin in cocaine shipments, and using brand names to build their client base and customer loyalty.

The South American and Latin American countries supplied 75 per cent of US heroin in 1997, 65 per cent in 1998 and around 60 per cent in 1999. Virtually all of the six tonnes/tons of heroin produced in Colombia during 1998 was believed to have been shipped to the US market, and Colombian heroin began to dominate the streets of east coast cities such as New York and Washington in 1999. The heroin trade in Colombia was in the hands of many independent trafficking groups and the drug is smuggled mainly in quantities of 1kg (21/4lb) or 2kg (41/2lb) by couriers on commercial airlines.

Criminal organizations based in Nigeria and West Africa, with drug connections in Southeast and Southwest Asia, also distributed heroin to some major cities in the United States, particularly the Chicago area. Similarly, nearly all heroin produced in Mexico between 1999 and 2001 was destined for US distribution. Mexican heroin, which accounted for 24 per cent of US seizures in 1999, became more popular in southwestern US cities such as San Diego and Los Angeles.

Evidence suggests that trafficking organizations from Mexico were attempting to produce higher-purity heroin in the late 1990s. A 1997 analysis of Mexican heroin distributed in the USA revealed purity levels of 30 to 60 per cent, with some samples reaching levels of more than 70 per cent.

HEROIN INJECTING, SMOKING AND SNORTING

Heroin is a very adaptable drug. Many narcotics can only be popped as pills or snorted. Heroin, however, can be administered in a variety of ways with different effects. It can be sniffed, smoked, swallowed or injected. These methods can involve different techniques. Heroin can be smoked though a water pipe or normal pipe (often glass), mixed with a marijuana joint, inhaled as smoke through a straw (chasing the dragon), snorted as a powder (commonly through a straw), or dissolved in water and injected under the skin, into muscles or intravenously (into a vein).

Sniffing or snorting is done in the same way as cocaine users do Charlie. The heroin is chopped with a blade, razor or credit card, drawn into lines and then snorted up one nostril with the aid of a rolled-up banknote or tube. The bitter flavour of heroin can put users off this method, and sniffing largely remains the preserve of the cocaine addict.

Swallowing heroin is pretty rare because it is an inefficient way of delivering a rush. The stomach converts heroin into morphine and the liver does a good job of breaking down the morphine before it can have an effect.

With smoking, a small amount of H is placed on a piece of aluminium foil and a flame held beneath it. As the drug is heated it turns black and wriggles like a snake. The resulting fumes are sucked up into the nose with the help of a tube.

INJECTING

Injection can be done in three ways:

- **Skin Popping** - The common name given to subcutaneous injection, which targets the fatty tissue lying just beneath the skin (usually in the buttocks, stomach or thighs);

LEEDS COLLEGE OF BUILDING
LIBRARY

The Little Book Of **HEROIN**

- **Intramuscular Injection** – When the user targets their large muscle groups, normally in the thigh, buttocks or the top of the arms;
- **Intravenous Injection** – Also called mainlining, which targets veins.

Typically, a heroin abuser will inject up to four times in a day. Mainlining directly into veins provides the greatest intensity and most rapid onset of euphoria (between seven and eight seconds), while intramuscular injection or skin popping produces a slower high, sometimes taking as long as eight minutes before the onset of euphoria.

When heroin is snorted or smoked, peak effects are usually much longer – taking between 10 and 15 minutes – and, in addition to a slower 'rush', these methods don't create the intensity of intravenous injection. All forms of heroin administration are addictive.

Intramuscular or subcutaneous injection was used almost exclusively in Britain in the early part of the 20th century. But intravenous use, which was more common in the USA, eventually spread to the UK and Europe around the 1950s, possibly because injection is the most practical and efficient way of administering low-purity heroin.

Intravenous use carries with it all the primary health risks facing heroin users. Mainlining means that any toxic substances cut with the drug are shot directly into the blood, leading to abscesses, blood poisoning or worse.

In the process of injecting heroin users will usually place a small amount of the drug (anything up to the size of a pea, although it varies enormously depending on the addict) on to a spoon. If they are fixing with brown they will add a drop of citric or ascorbic acid and water to help dissolve the heroin. Sometimes vinegar and lemon juice are more easily available for the junkie, but can cause infection.

The mix is heated over a naked flame from a lighter until it dissolves. Once the heroin has melted and cooled it can be drawn up into a syringe and injected. Often a small swab of cotton wool or a filter from a cigarette will also be used to screen some of the toxins in the heroin, but bacteria can still be drawn into the hypodermic.

At the start of a habit, the needle user will inject in the most accessible veins, which are the main arteries located in the inner portion of the arm near the elbow joint. Usually, a right-handed person will inject in the left arm and a left-handed person into the right arm. Sometimes injectors will also pump their arms or use a tourniquet such as a belt or tie to make a bigger target of the vein.

FIRST PERSON
LISA S, HEROIN ADDICT
'I started with a needle in the 1970s. I was 17 at the time and didn't know there was anything but mainlining. Also, I never smoked, never have, which is pretty unusual I guess with heroin users. My boyfriend at the time was a user and

he showed me what to do. He fixed me up with my first shot and I thought it was wonderful.

'You hear all these stories about people feeling bad and puking up. But that was not my experience. I thought it was really wonderful. I suppose I'd been around drugs quite a lot then and had tried most of everything, especially acid. I had the best two or three years of my life. Fantastic music, great gigs, and smack.

'There'd be some bad times where we couldn't get hold of any dope for a few days and then I couldn't cope. That was dreadful. I was working on the tills in a market, just a small corner convenience store really, but I just couldn't face it without a fix. I'd ring in at least once a week and tell them I was ill. I don't know if they suspected anything. I kept myself pretty presentable and it wasn't like there were many heroin addicts around then. I could fix myself and did sometimes, but mostly my boyfriend did it.

'What happened then was he had a terrible motorbike accident and was in hospital for nearly a year. The doctors got him off heroin while he was there and I started to visit him less and less because I was still doing it. Although, by this time my health was really shot. I'd miss veins and get bruising all over my arm. Then I met someone else who was also dealing a bit. He moved in and, although I knew he was ripping me off, we stuck together because of the dope I knew he could always get.

'By this time my veins were pretty fucked up. I was spilling loads of blood all over the place and the hits seemed to be becoming less and less. I just didn't get that feeling back. I don't know if it was the quality of the dope or something. So we both started doing cocaine as well. Around this time I realised I couldn't keep a lid on everything. I'd lost the supermarket job and was just doing odd shifts in a local bar.

'Then my first boyfriend came out of hospital and I saw him one night in another pub. Even though his leg was a bit fucked, he looked really good. He was completely clean and he'd been away on holiday somewhere and was suntanned, and that's what I noticed most, his skin and hair. Also, the idea of going away had never been something we would have done. In fact, I hardly recognized him because he'd been a user ever since I'd met him.

'He didn't give me any lecture, In fact I can't remember if we even spoke, but something clicked then and I knew I had to move out of the flat with the dealer. It probably took another two years to get off the gear altogether, but I've been clean since.'

SNIFFING AND SMOKING

In the 1980s and 1990s there was a shift in heroin-use patterns in some US cities and the UK: from injection to sniffing and smoking. Evidence suggests that heroin snorting is widespread in cities and countries where high-purity heroin is available. Snorting heroin is now the most widely reported means of taking heroin among users admitted for drug treatment in Newark, Chicago and New York.

Along with the shift in abuse patterns to new, young users lured by inexpensive, high-purity heroin that can be snorted or smoked, heroin has also been appearing in more affluent communities. In the past, groups such as students and business executives have traditionally avoided the drug because of negative images of needles and the stigma associated with track marks. However, smoking and snorting bypass this.

Snorting and smoking are also more appealing to a new group of users because these methods eliminate the fear of acquiring syringe-borne diseases such as HIV and hepatitis B and C.

When smoked, heroin is heated on a small piece of baking foil and the fumes inhaled through a tube. Chasing the dragon – so called because the smoke spiralling off the aluminium foil looks like a dragon's tail – became popular in 1980s Britain when fairly large supplies of heroin were flooding council estates in cities such as Liverpool, Manchester and London.

There is certainly less equipment necessary for chasing the dragon. The mainliner will have his 'works'. He needs to be able to cook up the dope, often using something like a rubber hose to tie off his arm and, most importantly, a working sterile syringe with a sharp needle.

The smoker only needs to rip off a piece of kitchen roll or buy some chocolate wrapped in silver foil – both easily available, cheap and reusable. However, there is some skill necessary with chasing. The user needs to be quick with their tube because if the heroin is heated too quickly smoke will be lost.

Chasing the dragon has one final, but important, advantage over mainlining: smokers can test the quality of the dope they are using. Mainliners will dissolve the dope, fix a shot and inject it. Only then will they know how pure the heroin is. Smokers have the chance to gradually discover the quality of the heroin they're taking by only lightly inhaling the first puff.

HEROIN SYRINGES

Syringes, needles. The works. Next to heroin itself, they are the most important part of the junkie's kit. Some junkies sleep with them. However, they can also be the weapon that finally kills them. Needles deliver the OD. They can also serve up HIV.

The threat of HIV in the early 1980s prompted action from governments and led to the introduction of pilot needle-exchange schemes in the UK in 1986. These, which have been followed by similar schemes in many other countries, allowed users to swap their old works for a new, clean syringe. By 1987, 15 needle-swap schemes were operating in UK cities such as Liverpool and Sheffield and, by 1991, some four million syringes were being distributed from around 200 swap agencies in the UK.

Needle exchanges are criticized by some politicians and pressure groups, who argue that they legitimize heroin consumption and encourage the most dangerous method of administration. There are also complaints from the local population, worried that needle exchanges will draw heroin addicts to their neighbourhood, resulting in it being littered with their dirty needles.

HEROIN ABUSE LEVELS

Heroin use is a global phenomenon – and problem. Of the 180 million people the United Nations estimates use an illegal drug, some 9.18 million around the world – or 0.22 per cent of the global population – were estimated to be heroin users in the late 1990s.

There are very few countries that heroin doesn't touch and infect with its attendant problems. This is demonstrated by the UN Office for Drug Control and Crime Prevention (ODCCP) World Drug Report 2000, which showed that of the 134 countries and territories surveyed, plant-based drugs such as the opiates, including heroin, were the most commonly abused. Some 76 per cent of those reported an abuse of heroin during the 1990s, significantly more than the 64 per cent and 24 per cent who reported cocaine and ecstasy abuse respectively.

The main regions of consumption are traditionally close

to the areas of production and the large markets. Thus the highest rates of abuse of heroin are mostly concentrated in Asia (the highest levels of abuse are in Iran, Pakistan, India, and the Lao PDR) and Europe, where 5.74 million and 1.5 million addicts respectively are believed to live.

PROFILE OF A HEROIN USER

Who takes heroin? Junkies, sure. But how does one brother in a stable middle-class family take up the needle, while the other becomes a journalist on a national newspaper?

It's more complicated than sociology, genetics and psychology can explain on their own, and clearly there are myriad reasons and influences that will persuade someone to use heroin. Environment, education, peer pressure, personality type and ease of availability of heroin all play a part.

Studies show that certain people are more susceptible to using drugs – and subsequently becoming dependent on them – than others. There is no standard heroin-using profile. Users come from all socio-economic groups and from a wide range of personality types and family backgrounds.

However, studies have identified a series of risk and protective factors which can work at various levels on the psychological development of an individual, including the local or family environment, the personality of the user and education. Generally the greater potential for drug misuse and escalation to dependence and addiction depends on the balance of risk and protective factors.

For example, risk factors in the environment will include a high prevalence of drug taking among peer groups and easy availability of drugs such as heroin in the user's area. Again, a depressed, sensation-seeking personality will also predict a risk that could lead the individual to seek out a drug like heroin. Against this, someone with high self-esteem and an easy temperament is perceived as having in-built protection against turning to heroin or other drugs.

Some attempt has also been made to create a picture of a typical heroin user, and a glimpse is provided by the 2001 study, Drug Misuse Declared In 2000: Results From The British Crime Survey (BCS). This outlined drug-use patterns among the population of England and Wales, and demonstrated that a young white man from Manchester with no academic qualifications is much more likely to become a junkie than a middle-class Pakistani woman from a rural background, who went to university.

Some experts believe this UK study can be extrapolated to provide a profile of the features of drug and heroin users in Europe and many other western countries. Drug Misuse Declared In 2000 showed that drug use was more prevalent among young people, with 50 per cent of 16- to 29-year-olds reporting that they have tried drugs in their lifetime.

The study also found that people tend to restrict their drug use to a single drug. In the last year, 15 per cent of

16- to 29-year-olds used one drug, compared to 4 per cent who had used two drugs.

Use of opiates, including heroin, crack and methadone, was relatively low compared to drugs like cannabis, ecstasy, LSD, and magic mushrooms. Only 5 per cent of 16- to 59-year-olds had tried opiates in their lifetime and, in the last year, only around 1 per cent of 16- to 29-year-olds had taken heroin and crack.

The survey also suggested that drug use is not spread evenly around the UK and that certain drugs are more popular in different regions. London tends to have the highest rates of drug use, with over 30 per cent of 16- to 29-year-olds reporting Class A drug use in the last year (of the study). That compared with about 20 per cent in Wales. However, in the same age group, use of heroin was highest in the north of England, the south and the Midlands with less than 0.5 per cent taking the drug in London and negligible usage in Wales.

The study also found that socio-economic factors – income level, education, type of neighbourhood – can contribute to drug usage and also influence the type of drug favoured. For instance, whereas cocaine use is relatively widespread across the whole population, heroin tends to be associated with less affluent groups. Very few 16- to 29-year-olds from affluent urban, suburban, rura, or family areas reported using heroin in 2001.

This relationship between heroin and the less affluent was reinforced by measuring use of heroin with factors such as income, qualifications and employment status. The proportion who used heroin in the last year was found to be highest in the poorest households – those earning less than £5,000 ($7,300) – among those with zero academic qualifications, the unskilled and the unemployed.

Heroin use in the UK has increased slightly since 1994 and the BCS 2000 survey showed that it is in the 16- to 29-year-old age group where the main increase has taken place. In 2000, 0.7 per cent of those surveyed in that age group said they had used heroin in the last year, compared to just 0.5 per cent in 1994 and 0.3 per cent in 1996.

The report shows that usage of the drug between genders has not shifted significantly over the years between 1994 and 2000, but rates of use of the drug in the last year for the unemployed were noticeably higher in 1998 and 2000 than for those in work.

Ethnic comparisons of drug use are also possible and the BCS 2000 survey found that, irrespective of age, white people were more likely to have taken drugs than black people, Indians or Pakistanis. Heroin, in particular, is almost unused in the UK among the latter two ethnic groups.

HEROIN PHYSIOLOGY

Heroin mimics the action of natural chemicals, called endorphins (endogenous morphines), which are produced in response to pain. They will act on specific opiate receptor sites in the brain and spinal cord to dampen the flow of nerve impulses in nerve tracts that carry pain information to the brain.

The opiate receptors – proteins embedded in the cell membrane – are not designed to recognize heroin, but are part of the human body's defence against pain and are normally activated by the endorphins. These chemicals are released in conditions of great stress and anxiety to 'cut off' pain, and explain why a soldier shot in battle may not immediately feel a wound or even realise that he has been hurt.

There are three different types of opiate receptor located in various parts of the human body and these will be activated by heroin entering the user's system. Those located in the brainstem are responsible for alerting the user to pain and one opiate receptor in particular – the mu-opioid receptor – is responsible for the pain-relieving and pleasurable effect of heroin. For example, if someone burns their finger on a hot saucepan, messages will be sent from the fingertips to the spinal cord, which telegraphs another message to the arm muscles to remove the hand – quickly. These are messages aimed at putting a direct stop to the painful stimuli.

However, to prevent the person from burning their fingers again, another signal is simultaneously sent from the spinal cord to the part of the opiate receptors in the brainstem, that will 'alarm' pain. However, the presence of opiates or heroin will remedy this through their analgesic effect. The feeling does not entirely disappear, but it loses its threatening character.

The critical aspect of heroin and other opiates is that this painkilling effect has little or no effect on other sensory perceptions such as motor functions and consciousness. This is very different from other non-opiate drugs, such as barbiturates, or substances like alcohol, which also have painkilling qualities, but will have a very significant effect on motor co-ordination, consciousness and intellectual capability. Although, at very high dosage levels, heroin can cause drowsiness.

Heroin does, however, have some major physical effects on other areas of the body. It can also have an effect on breathing because opiate receptors are also located in the respiratory centre. These are designed to regulate the frequency and beat of breathing, and allow steady inhalation depending on the level of exertion a person is experiencing. However, heroin will also have an inhibiting effect on these cells, often reducing the depth and frequency of someone's breathing. In the event of a heroin overdose, respiration will shut down completely. This will cause a shortage of oxygen to the brain and muscles and stop the heart.

Similarly, by influencing the hypothalmus, the area of the brain responsible for the hypophysis, controlling the body's hormonal balance, heroin can effect the levels of cortisol and testosterone in the blood and body temperature. This will decrease or increase slightly, depending on the dosage, but the affect may diminish through use and tolerance.

Opiate receptors can also cause vomiting. Normally stimulated by contaminated food, these cells are also pushed into activity by heroin, which explains why many first-time users throw up after a fix. Tolerance to this quickly builds, however, and it is unusual for regular users to vomit.

Heroin will also cause constipation because of the effect of opiates on the digestive system where many opiate receptors are also located. This is why opiates, which inhibit intestinal functioning, have been used as painkillers and for diarrhoea.

Another side effect of opiate use is that veins in the skin will be widened by the release of histamine. This has the result of giving the user a flushed and sweaty appearance, and it can also lead to constant itching.

The most visible and sometimes shocking side effect of heroin abuse is the effect on the pupils of the eye. They become like pinpoints, due to miosis (where the pupils contract), and this can happen almost immediately. This occurs even if the heroin user is fixing up in a darkened room, when the pupils are normally expected to become enlarged or dilated (mydriasis).

At the same time as creating euphoria by dampening distress, pain and other negative stimuli, heroin use can also lead to mood change. The opiate receptors in the limbic system can severely reduce the heroin user's appetite for sex. The signals to opiate receptors are not cut, but any cognitive link leads to total emotional indifference.

Heroin is the fastest-acting of all opiates. Its increased liquid solubility allows it to cross the blood-brain barrier rapidly and the drug is reconverted back to morphine before it binds to the opiate receptors.

The effect of the drug is essentially the same regardless of the method of administration. However, when injected intravenously it reaches the brain in seven to eight seconds. This is the 'rush', an intense sensation following injection. Intramuscular injections, or skin popping, produce a relatively slow onset of this euphoric feeling, taking between five and eight minutes. The peak experience through smoking or snorting can take up to 15 minutes.

Users will offer a variety of responses to heroin, but there will always tend to be three effects associated with heroin use: those that are sought-after, such as euphoria and the removal of tension, and then the short-term and long-term side effects of taking the drug. These can range from nausea to malnutrition.

The surge of pleasure – the rush or buzz – seems to start in the abdomen. A warmth then spreads throughout the body and with this a dissipation of pain, fear, hunger, aggression, frustration, tension and anxiety. The user will feel calm. Time may seem to slow down, users may feel that they have a dry mouth and their limbs become heavy.

I heard all this stuff about being in your mom's womb, you know like being in a warm place. Somewhere safe. Wrapped up in cotton wool, inside a big air bag. And they were right. That's exactly what heroin is.

– Kerry James, heroin user

The euphoria produced by heroin does not lead to a happy, smiling person. But it does remove the weight of the world from the user's shoulders. After the intense euphoria passes, users experience a period of tranquillity, sometimes referred to as 'being on the nod'. They will feel alternately drowsy and wakeful, warm and content, and may fall in and out of a sleeping state, often burning themselves or furniture if they are smoking a cigarette at the time. The narcotic power of the drug will diminish any feeling of pain if a user does injure themselves. Mental functioning can become clouded because of the depression of the central nervous system. This feeling can last for up to an hour or more.

Experienced heroin users will inject between two and four times each day. After taking heroin, some people feel cocooned and emotionally self-contained. Others feel stimulated and sociable. Either way, there is a profound sense of control, and heroin also detaches the user from any feelings of pain or worry. They will also have slowed and slurred speech, a slow gait, constricted pupils, droopy eyelids and impaired night vision.

The euphoria gradually subsides into a dreamy and relaxed state of contentment. Higher doses of heroin normally make users very sleepy and very high doses will cause the user to slip into a semi-conscious state. The effects will wear off in three to five hours, again depending on the dosage.

HEROIN HEALTH

Heroin is not associated with good health. It's perceived as dirty and dangerous. Evil in a needle. In an ICM Research poll conducted for the UK's *Observer* newspaper in February and March 2002, 27 per cent believed that heroin was the drug likely to cause the greatest risk to health. Crack came in second at 19 per cent.

However, heroin has had a bad press. Unlike many narcotics, the drug is actually benign and there is little evidence to suggest that a lifetime of using pure dope would lead to anything more than a strong tolerance to the drug. This could lead to serious problems of dependency and withdrawal, but the real medical concerns that arise from chronic heroin use are due to other factors. These include adulterants in the dope, infected hypodermic syringes, the environment and habits of the addict, and methods of administration. Because the heroin abuser is always on the lookout for their next fix, they often neglects the normal necessary functions that people take for granted, such as eating and sleeping, and health problems set in through their general run-down condition. Spending any spare cash on drugs also means that their living conditions and diet are likely to be poor.

Initially, a new user will be recognized by their pale or jaundiced complexion and dramatic weight loss. The myriad complications associated with longer-term use include septicaemia, pulmonary abscesses and skin abscesses, and a long-term user may also find that the veins they use to inject become scarred or collapse, and they will have to find new veins to inject.

Chronic users may also develop bacterial infection of the blood vessels, infection of the heart lining and valves, cellulitis and liver disease. Pulmonary complications, including a number of different types of pneumonia, may result from the poor health condition of the abuser as well as from heroin's depressing effects on respiration. Long-term physical effects can also result in respiratory system problems – breathlessness is a common complaint, as is coughing up phlegm – and chronic sedation.

Pure, unadulterated heroin does no damage to the body's organs. However, street heroin may have additives that do not really dissolve, resulting in clogging of the blood vessels that lead to the lungs, liver, kidneys or brain. This can cause infection or even the death of small patches of cells in vital organs. Immune reactions to contaminants can also cause arthritis and other rheumatological problems.

Users also risk overdosing (ODing) because heroin is generally obtained from illegal suppliers and, therefore, the dose is unpredictable and may be dangerously adulterated by the dealer. An overdose (OD) will cause rapid heartbeat, heart failure, shortness of breath, ringing in the ears or head, pin-point pupils, clammy skin, convulsions, unconsciousness and coma. When unconscious, users also risk the danger of choking on their own vomit.

Protracted use also causes extreme constipation and a loss of appetite. This can lead to malnutrition in addicts because they are never hungry and because the constipation can become so painful that they do not want to eat food.

Mental health problems can also result. Addiction and the psychological symptoms of withdrawal include depression, mood swings, and hypersensitivity to pain. The user will also lose their appetite for sex.

Abuse can also cause additional complications for women, whose livers are smaller than men's and will therefore be placed under more strain. Menstrual irregularity is likely and some women will cease ovulation. Pregnant drug users also risk miscarriage, stillbirth, or giving birth to smaller babies as a result of retarded growth in the womb or premature delivery. Congenital abnormalities are also common; they often exhibit a number of developmental problems and are at greater risk of cot death or SIDS (Sudden Infant Death Syndrome).

Pregnant abusers can also cause irreparable damage if they suddenly withdraw from heroin, although it is very common that the baby will experience withdrawal symptoms after birth. Symptoms can vary enormously, but usually the baby will be hyperactive and restless. Sometimes the infant may even go into seizure, but often these effects can be minimized by a programme of tranquillizers such as chlorpromazine or benzodiazepine.

PHARMACOLOGICAL EFFECTS
DESIRED
- Warmth
- Sense of well-being and contentment
- Detachment from physical and emotion distress
- Relief from pain
- Reduced levels of tension and anxiety.

SHORT TERM
- Nausea
- Vomiting

- Drowsiness
- Apathy and inability to concentrate
- Constricted pupils
- Death if respiratory depression caused by overdose

LONG TERM
- Diminished appetite leading to weight loss and malnutrition
- Constipation
- Abscesses, if injected
- HIV
- Irregular periods
- Physical and psychological dependence
- Increased tolerance
- Chronic sedation
- Withdrawal symptoms, including sweating, chills, cramps, and diarrhoea

Potentially the most serious health risk to heroin addicts is that of contracting human immunodeficiency virus (HIV), hepatitis C and other infectious diseases through sharing and re-use of infected needles and injection paraphernalia. Drug abusers may also become infected through unprotected sexual contact with an infected person.

HIV is responsible for AIDS, and takes hold by attacking the immune system – the T-cells – of its host, which are normally responsible for fighting infection. HIV gradually destroys the ability of the immune system to mount a defence against other viruses or infections. Reported HIV incidence among those using heroin, and other injecting drug users (IDUs), is now a worldwide problem affecting countries from Australia to Argentina.

The UN Office for Drug Control and Crime Prevention report Global Illicit Drug Trends 2000 stated that the practice of injecting heroin and other drugs was also spreading to developing countries and taking the HIV virus with it. It blamed injection drug use (IDU) as the major, if not the main, mode of transmission for HIV infection in North Africa, the Middle East, East Asia, Latin America, eastern Europe, Central Asia, western Europe and North America. In the USA, it is thought that IDU has been a factor in an estimated one-third of all HIV and more than half of all hepatitis C cases.

In 1999 the steepest HIV curve was found in the former states of the Soviet Union. The virus is understood to have spread from the Ukraine in the mid-1990s to the Baltic states, the Caucasus and Central Asia, where IDU is perceived as the primary cause of HIV. In Moscow alone, in 1999, 2,700 new HIV cases were reported, three times as many as in all previous years combined; a high proportion of these were blamed on heroin users fixing up.

Other central and eastern European countries believed by the report to be at risk from the HIV epidemic spread by IDUs are the Czech Republic, and Serbia and Montenegro.

Drug injection - and HIV - was also believed to be on the increase in China and Myanmar, where it was understood to be diffusing from urban to rural areas. Heroin injection, already established in Hong Kong and Thailand, was also reported to be spreading to Vietnam and Lao PDR. In 1995 it was estimated that 77 per cent of HIV infections in Malaysia were among IDUs.

In Australia, heroin is the most commonly injected drug and HIV prevalence among IDUs is less than 5 per cent. The number of people with HIV in Austria is thought to be between 12,000 and 14,000, nearly half of whom are drug users. HIV infection in Austria among drug users varies from around 12-30 per cent in Vienna to 50 per cent in western parts of the country.

In the UK, the spread of HIV among heroin users and other IDUs has been largely stopped because of the success of the mid-1980s decision to implement a policy of clean needles. By March 1999 almost 3,500 drug injectors had tested positive for HIV, and more than 1,000 had been diagnosed with AIDS. However, drug researchers believe this has abated.

Research has also discovered that drug abusers can change their risk-taking behaviour - sharing syringes, unsafe sexual practices and so on - through drug-abuse treatment, prevention, and community-based outreach programmes.

Sharing needles also puts the heroin user at risk of hepatitis, a viral infection that attacks the liver and has affected the drug-injecting community for longer than HIV. There are three strains of hepatitis:

- **Hepatitis A** – Associated with poor hygiene, and spread through water and food contamination
- **Hepatitis B** and **C** – Most relevant to injectors.

Hepatitis B is transmitted through blood, but can also be passed though saliva and semen. It incubates for around three months before exhibiting a range of flu-like symptoms. The virus will clear up and a full recovery is normally expected in around six months.

Hepatitis C (HCV) is probably the most serious form of hepatitis and, unlike hepatitis A, can lead to chronic liver damage in 70 per cent of sufferers, and sometimes death. It is estimated to have infected around 35,000 people in the UK alone and although it is impossible to put a figure on the number of those infected through heroin use, it is likely to be in the low thousands. The disease kills about 8,000 people annually in the USA, and about 3.9 million Americans are believed to be infected with the virus. By 2010 it is estimated that up to 39,000 people in the USA will die from the disease each year.

However, it is not necessary for the heroin addict to have shared a needle with a hepatitis C sufferer. The National Center for Infectious Diseases warns that the sharing of any drug equipment, such as razors or mirrors, can potentially be harmful.

What makes the virus particularly difficult to diagnose is that around 80 per cent of those with hepatitis C do not display any symptoms. Those that do will experience flu-like aches, fatigue, jaundice, diarrhoea, abdominal pain and loss of appetite. Around one-fifth of sufferers will clear the virus from their systems in up to 12 months, but in others the disease can remain dormant for anything up to 30 years and by that time irreversible liver damage may have been done.

> I think I got it [hepatitis C] from dirty needles in the
> 1980s and it means I've had to give up any hard drinking.
> I can just about manage a pint of cider every so often,
> but that's against doctor's advice. Hepatitis has really
> fucked me up physically.
> 							 - Lee M, heroin addict with hepatitis C

It is estimated that some 40 per cent of hepatitis C patients can be successfully treated with recent advances in medication administered for the disease. Alpha interferon (IFN-alpha) alone, or in combination with oral ribavirin, is commonly used and combination therapy (interferon plus ribavirin) is rapidly superseding interferon monotherapy because this dual therapy is significantly more effective.

The standard interferon regimen for patients with chronic hepatitis C consists of three IFN-alpha injections per week for up to 18 months. Some 40 per cent of patients treated with IFN-alpha alone can retain normalized liver function.

Treatment with interferon leads to a variety of side effects, which can significantly impair quality of life. Some clinical trials suggest that over 60 per cent of patients treated with IFN have influenza-like symptoms. Other common and disabling side effects are chronic fatigue and depression.

Treatment with IFN and ribavirin is effective in clearing HCV in almost 40 per cent of treated patients. However, combination therapy is expensive and carries significant side effects, particularly anaemia, depression and weight loss.

The ultimate price to pay for using heroin is death. Many heroin deaths are through suffocation, usually if the user's air passages are blocked by vomit and they have fallen asleep or slipped into unconsciousness.

OD

Overdose of heroin – OD, or dropping – when the body hasn't built enough tolerance to cope with the quantity of heroin taken, is another frequent danger. Overdose is very common and even small amounts of heroin may cause some people to OD after a period of non-use. This often happens if an addict has been in prison or hospital: when they return to heroin and pump their normal dose into a vein, the body can't cope. Sometimes junkies can simply take too much, perhaps because they have a supply from a new source, or the heroin they score could be significantly purer than the cut dope they regularly inject.

PHYSICAL SYMPTOMS OF HEROIN OD

- Abnormal or very slow breathing
- Cold skin and low body temperature
- Slow heartbeat
- Muscle twitching
- Slow working of the central nervous system
- Gurgling sound in the throat from vomit or saliva
- Blue tips of fingernails and toenails because of low oxygen
- Small pupils
- Drowsiness
- Unconsciousness
- Coma

An OD victim may go into a coma or die. OD death - or in junkie argot, pulling a blue one or bluey - can take the form of heart failure, liver failure or respiratory failure. The physical symptoms of a fatal heroin dose will start with slow, shallow breathing and the pupils will turn to pinpoints. Blood pressure will drop alarmingly, the skin will turn blue and the OD victim will slip into unconsciousness and coma. Death can be almost immediate or the whole process can take up to ten hours.

The best way of preventing overdose is not to use heroin alone, and many users have buddies to fix up with. Neither should heroin be used in tandem with alcohol, tranquillizers or other drugs, and if the drug has been bought from a new dealer, a small amount should be tried first to test how pure the heroin is. Antagonists, which block the action of opioids such as naloxone, can also sometimes reverse the effects of OD.

OD DOS AND DON'TS

DO

- Phone an ambulance immediately and tell the operator that the person has overdosed
- Stay with the OD victim
- Keep the OD victim awake by walking them around and talking to them
- If the OD victim is unconscious, put them in the recovery position
- Check their breathing and clear their airway
- Administer mouth-to-mouth resuscitation if they stop breathing

DON'T

- Inject the person with any other drug

- Put them under the shower
- Put anything in their mouth

Real problems can also result if the injector hits an artery (arteries take blood away from the heart, whereas veins return the blood to the heart). Sometimes the plunger in the syringe will be forced back by the high pressure of the blood and rapid bleeding will result; this will need urgent attention, otherwise it can result in the loss of limbs and sometimes death.

It is almost impossible to get accurate statistics on heroin-related deaths, because the definition of heroin-related deaths is potentially very wide. It could, for example, include accidental overdose, suicides through overdose, poisoned heroin, accidental death while under the influence of heroin, death from AIDS after contracting the HIV virus through injecting heroin, and murder or manslaughter while under the influence of heroin.

Often, doctors will record the cause of death without making any mention of the drug in the system. However, the UK's Office for National Statistics (ONS) has estimated the number of drug-related deaths for England and Wales (see table opposite), which includes accidental and deliberate narcotic overdose (excluding paracetamol). In 1993 there were about 900 deaths caused through drug abuse, rising to just over 1,700 in 1997. Of these, 255 were directly related to heroin and another 421 were linked with methadone, commonly used by heroin addicts to break their dependence. There were 38 deaths caused by cocaine and 12 through ecstasy use.

Further research implicated heroin and morphine in 43 per cent of the 1,296 drug-related deaths during 2000 in England and Wales, which suggested that the number of heroin deaths had risen by one third to 551. Many of the heroin-related deaths were caused because users had taken a cocktail of drugs, and the statistics appear to show that 'most at risk' is the heroin addict.

DRUG-RELATED DEATHS	
DRUG TYPE	NUMBER OF DEATHS
Methadone	421
Heroin	255
Temazepam	104
Amphetamines	40
Cocaine	38
Ecstasy	12

Source: Office for National Statistics, 1997

Heroin deaths also appear to be on the increase, around the world. In Australia there were just six in 1964 compared to 600 in 1997. Austria reported 86 drug-related deaths in 1988 and Belgium had 91 drug deaths in 1990, most through heroin abuse.

HEROIN ADDICTION

Addiction or dependence means that a large part of a

LEEDS COLLEGE OF BUILDING
LIBRARY

person's life is governed by drugs. Buying them and taking them. It is a chronic, relapsing disease, characterized by compulsive drug seeking and use, and by neurochemical and molecular changes in the brain.

And it's a growing problem. Dependence – a strong compulsion to keep taking drugs – is an insidious aspect of any recreational abuse. UK charity group Action on Addiction estimates that around one in three adults in the UK suffers from some form of addiction, costing the tax-payer around £5 billion ($7.25 billion) in 2002.

Not all drugs are as addictive as others. Many drugs users can drink alcohol and then not touch a drop of the hard stuff for months. And US research, available through the American National Comorbidity Survey, demonstrates that cannabis has a very low potential for dependence.

Heroin is a different matter. Heroin produces profound degrees of tolerance and physical dependence, which are also powerful motivating factors for compulsive use and abuse. As with abusers of any addictive drug, heroin abusers gradually spend more and more time and energy obtaining and using the drug. Once they are addicted, the heroin abuser's brain becomes wired to that drug and their primary purpose in life is to seek out and use more and more heroin. (Physical dependence is not inevitable, however, and some heroin users are able to take it on an occasional basis.)

Although heroin is not used as widely as many other drugs, such as tobacco or alcohol, once tried, a very high proportion of users will go on to use it regularly: they will become totally dependent on it. They will be addicted, and dependence is one of the main characteristics that pervades heroin use and informs treatment for the drug.

One symptom of heroin use is physical dependence, which does not occur with ecstasy, LSD or softer drugs like cannabis. This results from repeated, heavy use of the drug and can alter the body chemistry, building up tolerance to the drug. The body adapts to the presence of the drug and withdrawal symptoms occur if use is reduced abruptly. Withdrawal may occur within a few hours after the last time the drug is taken. With regular heroin use, tolerance develops. This means the user must use more and more heroin to achieve the same intensity or effect.

Withdrawal symptoms will occur if use is reduced or stopped. Withdrawal begins between 8 and 24 hours after the last fix and the symptoms are muscle aches, diarrhoea, cold flushes, goose bumps (cold turkey) and tremors, sweating, chills, runny nose, nausea, insomnia, muscular spasms, kicking movements ('kicking the habit'), yawning and sneezing. Elevation in blood pressure, pulse, respiratory rate and temperature occurs as withdrawal progresses. These effects will fade after a week to ten days, but a feeling of weakness may persist for several months after quitting the drug.

Major withdrawal symptoms peak between 24 and 48 hours after the last dose of heroin and subside after about a week. However, some people have shown persistent withdrawal signs for many months. Heroin withdrawal is never fatal to otherwise healthy adults, but it can cause death to the foetus of a pregnant addict.

Tolerance develops to the respiratory depressant, sedative, analgesic, emetic and euphoric effect through heroin use, so addicts will need to inject increased dosages to achieve the same effect they did weeks, months or years before, and if they terminate use they will suffer withdrawal effects. Sometimes addicted individuals will endure many of the withdrawal symptoms to reduce their tolerance for the drug so that they can again experience the initial rush.

Craving and relapse can occur weeks and months after withdrawal symptoms are long gone. However, patients with chronic pain who need opiates to function (sometimes over extended periods) have few if any problems leaving opiates after their pain is resolved by other means. This may be because the patient is simply seeking relief of pain and not the rush sought by the addict.

At the same time, the heroin addict will also evolve a psychological dependency, which is more common with users of other drugs. Essentially, this means the person using the drug feels they are unable to cope with the world unless they are under the influence of heroin, and friends, family and activities such as work take a secondary role.

Heroin dependency will often include both physical and psychological factors, and this has helped to produce more accurate definitions of drug dependence. Historically they have been framed in pejorative terms because early thinking tended to perceive addiction as simply a physical concept – a vice. More recently, psychological dependence has played a greater role. An expert committee working for the UN Commission on Narcotics in the early 1950s stated that addiction characteristics included an 'overpowering desire or need to continue taking the drug and to obtain it by any means; a tendency to increase the dose; a psychological and sometimes a physical dependence on the effects'. This differs markedly from a description of a habit-forming drug, which is generally understood to mean a narcotic that can be taken repeatedly without creating the bonds evident in addiction and that doesn't adversely affect the user.

In her 1999 account of her own experiences with the drug, *How To Stop Time: Heroin From A To Z*, Ann Marlowe attempts to explain her dependence to addicts as being similar to the satisfaction they will experience with their first coffee of the day. Subsequent coffees will never be the same. Marlowe wrote, 'The chemistry of the drug is ruthless: it is designed to disappoint you. Yes, once in a while there's a night when you get exactly where you're trying to go. Magic. Then you chase that memory for a month', adding that her definition of heroin addiction would be 'a form of mourning for the irrecoverable glories of the first time'.

The intensity of the intravenous high created through heroin means it is very likely that recreational use of the drug will lead to physical addiction and dependence. Heroin's ability to create dependence is neatly summed up in the table below, which shows the use of five drugs by a US sample group and the proportion of those who developed a dependence. Alcohol was the most commonly used, with 91.5 per cent of the US Household Survey admitting its use. However, transition from use to dependence for alcohol was relatively low with only 14.1 per cent developing an addiction.

At the other end of the scale, only 1.5 per cent of those surveyed had tried heroin, but of those 0.4 per cent developed an addiction. Thus, almost a quarter of those who do try the drug will end up with an addiction. That compares with less than 1 in 10 of people who develop an addiction to cannabis, despite it having been tried by approximately 30 times more people.

DEPENDENCE

Drug	Proportion of population who have used	Proportion who have developed dependence	Proportion of dependence
Tobacco	75.6%	24.1%	31.9%
Heroin	1.5%	0.4%	23.1%
Cocaine	16.2%	2.7%	16.7%
Alcohol	91.5%	14.1%	15.4%
Cannabis	46.3%	4.2%	9.1%

Source: US Household Survey

HEROIN PREVENTION

Preventing people from becoming heroin addicts in the first place is an objective of all governments attempting to contain their drug problems. If they are successful at stopping new users adopting heroin, their countries' injecting and smoking population will gradually reduce to zero.

Unfortunately, most drug experts concede that until prevention models become more complex to match the social factors being brought to bear on a heroin user, they will have only moderate success. History seems to support this view because prevention methods have had little or no effect on stopping the growth of the world's heroin problem.

DRUG PREVENTION AND EDUCATION

- Drug education has limited effect on behaviour and is unlikely to prevent teenagers from experimenting with drugs
- Education can increase knowledge, but strategies need to be based on a range of consistent approaches
- Education can contribute towards increased safety
- Shock tactics are generally believed to be counter-productive
- Measuring the effectiveness of drug prevention programmes is very difficult
- Prevention is neither a cheap nor easy option

Drug prevention is about raising knowledge and awareness which, given enough resources, are achievable objectives. However, in tandem with increasing information about heroin, is the objective to change behaviour. Harry Shapiro, communications director at UK drug resource DrugScope, says this is the hard part, 'It is very difficult to do. How can you get people to change their habits? There is a very rapid decay factor with information campaigns, a couple of weeks later people forget all about it.' However, Shapiro believes that the messages can sometimes sink in over time in the way that 'it has now become a lot less fashionable to drink and drive'.

What is clear is that the most effective prevention messages are those that have clear, well-defined aims, are relevant to the audience, and are sustained and consistent. Prevention strategy can encompass a wide range of tools to help deliver this. In the UK the Drug Prevention Advisory Service (DPAS) was established as an interface between the government and offices that can deliver prevention. It ensures that all prevention material and information conform to the four strands of the UK's anti-drugs strategy, which includes education and prevention.

EFFECTIVE HEROIN PREVENTION
- Should have a well-defined purpose
- Needs to be relevant to the audience
- Should include the most accurate and the most up-to-

the-minute information
- The messages need to be credible and delivered through credible sources such as youth services
- They should also challenge stereotypes
- Delivery needs to be through a well-thought-out plan, repeated often, but in a variety of imaginative ways
- Should be built on existing values and should reinforce existing anti-drug beliefs

At one end of the scale, prevention may also include harm-reduction approaches, which are particularly appropriate for needle-using heroin users. These might include prevention strategies to reduce the likelihood of succumbing to a drug overdose by offering resuscitation and awareness training to addicts or providing more access to methadone treatment, the established medication of choice for treating heroin addiction.

Prevention could also involve reducing the risk of HIV or hepatitis and will include the provision of information on sterilizing injecting equipment and making clean syringes more widely available.

An August 2001 consultation document addressing drug-prevention approaches suggested that the routes leading users towards heroin and addiction are so complex that several prevention strategies need to be developed.

Written by David Best and John Witton of the UK's National Addiction Centre, *Guidelines For Drug Prevention* suggested that prevention programmes can fall into two distinct groups: universal and targeted programmes. The former approach aims to reach the general population or a wide cross-section of society, and will include awareness campaigns and anti-drug education programmes, possibly at school.

The elements of school prevention are essentially the same throughout the world and will include a mix of drug-education classes and school visits by drug experts, social workers, former users or law enforcement. Results from the USA show that because two-thirds of all initiation to drug use in 1998 took place mostly during the school years – 12 to 17 years old – substance-prevention programmes in the classroom are vital.

However, Shapiro admits that the quality of drug information in schools varies enormously 'from the local police officer coming in for a chat, to the school putting on a play about the issues'. The level that messages should be pitched at is also hard to gauge because, within a class of 30 children, some will know nothing about drugs, some may be using drugs and others will think they know everything, but probably don't. Drug information in schools also flies in the face of how kids are normally taught. They are presented with drug information and asked to make up their own minds, but throughout the rest of the school curriculum they are told exactly what to do and how to behave.

There is a school of thought that prevention strategy in classrooms should accept drug experimentation as a given and concentrate mostly on how children can protect themselves and be safe if they use drugs. Shapiro accepts this is an option, but says the moral climate and opposition from some politicians, parents and teachers means that is unlikely to be accepted in the short term. 'I'm not sure teachers are going to be comfortable teaching kids how to inject,' he says.

Presenting a credible message to media-savvy children is also a problem faced by teachers. Gary Sutton, heroin project adviser at Release, doesn't believe enough is made of former drug addicts going into schools. Sutton argues that at the very least they can provide a credible message because they have been through heroin addiction, but believes the problem for schools asking outsiders to come in is that this may be seen as a tacit admission that the school has a drug problem. Sutton adds, 'Unless there is a borough-wide policy, then certain headmasters will be nervous because the implication of having a drug addict visit is that heroin or other drugs are used at that school and that has obvious implications for parents and school governors.'

Media campaigns also fall within the universal programme, and their role in drug prevention is to inform people about the services on offer, influence opinion formers and also create a climate where drugs are discussed.

However, there has been extensive debate about the use and effectiveness of campaigns, especially in the UK.

The UK's first national drug campaign came about in the mid-1980s. It featured heroin. Prior to that, heroin wasn't seen as being near the top of the political agenda because until the late 1970s there was a fairly stable and older injecting community. However, in the early 1980s there was an influx of smokable heroin.

The response of the Conservative government, in 1984, was to create a ministerial group chaired by the then Home Office minister David Mellor to create a strategy to stamp out heroin. This sparked one of the most high-profile and controversial episodes of Prime Minister Margaret Thatcher's political reign. The Department of Health and Social Security (DHSS) and the Central Office of Information (COI) approached Yellowhammer, an ambitious advertising agency based in London's West End, to produce a high-profile poster and press campaign aimed specifically at heroin users.

The images the agency produced were designed to shock. Under the white-on-black strapline 'Heroin Screws You Up', one showed a teenager in jeans and sweat-soaked shirt hunched up, his mouth pressed against his filthy hands and fingernails. 'Your Mind Isn't The Only Thing Heroin Damages' it warned, alongside seven well-documented by-products of heavy heroin use, including skin infections, wasted muscles and liver complaints. The copy was equally hard-hitting: 'You'll begin to take heroin not to get high any more, but just to feel normal. And, as you lose control of your body's health, you could lose control of your mind too. Until one day you'll wake up knowing that, instead of you controlling heroin, it now controls you.'

The same image accompanied by the same side effects – mental problems, skin infections, blood diseases, constipation – associated with long-term heroin addicts was given another eye-catching strapline – 'How Low Can You Get On Heroin?' – followed by the no-holds-barred copy 'Take heroin and before long you'll start looking ill, losing weight and feeling like death. So, if you're offered heroin, you know what to say.'

Another teenager, with dark rings under his eyes, spotty skin and a lank fringe, peered from another bleak ad. This strapline read 'Skin Care By Heroin'. Other ads used another withdrawn-looking male model and the line 'All He Wanted Was A Few Laughs'; one of the few ads using a female model had the copyline 'How You React Could Decide Whether She Rejects Drugs Or You'. Later the campaign was used in women's magazines to target mothers, whom the agency had identified in its research as the most important figure in the family for dealing with drug-related problems.

The campaign appeared at the same time as the street price of heroin had fallen, making heroin cheaper than some soft drugs and bringing in a new market of kids willing to smoke the drug. Few campaigns have attracted as much public attention as the £2 million ($2.9 million)

Yellowhammer campaign, which appealed to adolescent vanity. At the time Sammy Harari, the board account director at the ad agency, said, 'All this campaign is trying to do is to begin to shift people's attitudes.'

THE 'HEROIN SCREWS YOU UP' ADVERTISING CAMPAIGN
ARGUMENTS FOR
- Used as effective part of overall drug strategy, advertising is a persuasive instrument
- Helps increase information provision
- Is high profile

ARGUMENTS AGAINST
- Advertising has no effect on behaviour
- Unable to reach target groups
- Seems to be 'marketing' drugs
- Simplistic
- Glamorizes heroin and encourages anti-establishment teenagers to try it

The advantages of advertising and other universal programmes are that they don't label or stigmatize individuals and they may provide the groundwork for targeted programmes. However, it is often difficult to measure the effectiveness of broad prevention strategies and there doesn't appear to be any robust scientific evidence to show they work or have any lasting impact.

Drug experts suggested that the 'Heroin Screws You Up' campaign, for example, would only put off people who wouldn't try the drug anyway and wouldn't necessarily impact that much on those people who are already using. In other words, it may have the greatest effect on those at lowest risk.

The advertising also drew criticism from drug-charity workers and other experts, who thought that it may actually be counter-productive because young people would be drawn to the grunge images. They argued that the ad campaign was too simplistic because the posters gave the impression that people end up a mess if they take heroin, whereas the reality is that heroin is just one part of a combination of factors including drink and social circumstance. Therefore, they argued that it is better to spend the money on education in schools and throughout communities because then subtleties can be raised and understood.

The campaign also caused some problems for health workers. It scared many parents who thought that the onset of spots on their teenager's face meant they were on heroin. Heroin was being blamed for every problem in a family, even if no member of that family was actually taking it.

Significantly, this kind of campaign may also have the opposite effect to that it sets out to achieve. Teenagers are predominantly anti-Establishment, and there was anecdotal evidence that many found the emaciated models accompanied by the tough copylines attractive because they were seen as a product of the Establishment machine. The poster featuring the adolescent boy was a favourite of students, who hung it in their bedrooms next to posters of Nick Cave and David Bowie.

DEAD RINGERS

More recently, a UK media campaign featuring a young victim of heroin put the drug on the political agenda again. It showed the corpse of Rachel Whitear, which had lain slumped in a bedsit for several days after she had suffered an overdose. The image was undeniably powerful and garnered extensive national coverage on television and in newspapers.

However, there were many dissenting voices. Opponents of this and similar shock tactics argue it is scattergun scaremongering, rarely targeting users or potential users or communicating hard information about minimizing the effects of the drug or treatment. Also, because several similar campaigns have targeted heroin, some drug experts believe they give the impression that other Class A drugs, such as cocaine, are less harmful.

Thinking about prevention tactics in the early 2000s began to swing towards more targeted programmes, which aim to reduce the influence of the risk factors that lead people to heroin and build on creating coping strategies or other skills. Shapiro says, 'This one-size-fits-all campaign improves the profile of things, but it doesn't have that much impact. People don't change until they see they are at immediate risk.'

Best and Witton also believe targeted prevention programmes will single out the individuals who are most susceptible to drug misuse and suggest they have the potential to catch misuse early and are an efficient tool for directing resources to tackle the problem.

However, the biggest headaches arising from these methods are the difficulties associated with accurate targeting, cost and increasing the risk of stigmatization. They also ignore the wider social context that has led a user to drugs.

Targeted approaches can again encompass a wide variety of projects and drug support groups. For some heroin users they may involve the family or peer group. For example, if it is discovered that the addict is taking heroin because of pressure from friends, then a project could be developed to remove or reduce peer-group influence.

Sutton adds that both universal and targeted approaches always need to be used in conjunction with one another. 'We need to offer alternatives,' he says. 'Not just for preventing heroin use, because people drift into drug use because they don't have anything else in their lives. The alternative is to provide a different path, but of course it is very expensive to provide youth clubs and activities, which give young people a direction.'

Evidence from the US does seem to suggest that mass-media prevention campaigns are having some success. Following the United Nations Drug Control Program's (UNDCP) 1997 $200 million (£138 million) National Youth Anti-Drug Campaign, which used more targeted approaches, drug use in US schools fell away from an alarming upward swing. The Monitoring the Future studies group, which collects data on US school students, found that drug use among 14-year-old eighth-grade students fell in the USA between 1996 and 1999 by 12 per cent.

FIRST PERSON
MARK MCLEAN: UK NATIONAL DRUGS HELPLINE MANAGER
'We receive between 250,000 and 300,000 calls each year. It's a free and confidential service and then the National Drugs Helpline (NDH) refers one in five callers to drug agencies.

'We take more calls about heroin than any other drug. I'd say a quarter of our calls relate to heroin. After the death of Rachel Whitear we had lots of calls from parents. Parents respond more to stories like this than young people. Our remit is not to lobby the government or influence policy. We're like an older brother or sister to the young people who contact us. We're not judgmental, we don't tell them to get off drugs. We point out the legal risks and health risks associated with heroin or any other drug. People are going to take heroin anyway and our job is to advise them how to inject, to use clean needles, to avoid contaminated heroin, and also how to minimize harm.

'Campaigns like the "Heroin Screws You Up" advertising have the government stamped all over them, and for that reason are less credible among young people. The face of the person on the poster doesn't match the face of their mate who uses heroin so they aren't likely to trust the campaign.

'"Heroin Screws You Up" had an impact because people still remember it, but whether it has an impact on behaviour is debatable. The key for the campaigns we're involved in is to promote the services we offer and for that reason campaigns have to be credible and constructive, and direct people to information and support.'

HEROIN TREATMENT

When governments construct their drug budgets there is always a trade-off between how much they will spend on treatment and the resources put into tackling drug crime. For most of the last century, law and order has been the priority and so in the UK in 1998 only 13 per cent of the £1.4 billion ($2 billion) spent on drug-related activity went towards treatment.

However, the amount spent on treatment in most countries is generally increasing, boosted by the growing conviction that there is a better chance of winning the war on drugs if addicts are given treatment instead of punishment. Results from the USA also back up those who favour treatment over legislation. The US SAMHSA National Treatment Improvement Study 1996, which investigated the effectiveness of publicly funded drug treatment, discovered that there was a 47 per cent decline in heroin use one year after treatment ended.

Another US report, the Drug Abuse Treatment Outcome Studies conducted on behalf of the USA National Institute on Drug Abuse (NIDA) in the 1990s, also confirmed that treatment could significantly curb hardcore heroin use. One year after the end of treatment the study found that consumption levels of heroin had fallen by about two-thirds. In May 2002, the UK's Association of Chief Police Officers (ACPO) issued new proposals suggesting that, in some circumstances, treatment for heroin addiction should be considered as an alternative to prosecution. The ACPO report said it looked forward to the time when those who appear in court for misuse of Class A drugs, such as heroin, have immediate access to treatment.

Spending on drugs misuse in the UK was £700 million ($1 billion) in 2000/01 and expected to rise to £1 billion ($1.5 billion) in 2003/04. Of this, £234 million ($340 million) was spent on treatment in 2001/02, rising to over £400 million ($580 million) in 2003/04. Of this, the UK's National Treatment Agency (NTA), which is a joint initiative between the Home Office and the National Health Service to improve the quality and quantity of drug treatment, had a £234 million ($340 million) annual budget. By 2003 the NTA was expecting to have £400 million ($580 million) to spend on treatment, with funds significantly increasing until 2008.

In addition to this, £32 million ($46.5 million) was spent on young people and prevention work in 2001/02, due to rise to £71 million ($103 million) in 2003/04.

Any intervention – from providing better housing to creating jobs – that makes someone less likely to use heroin can be defined as treatment. However, health organizations normally focus on a much narrower definition of treatment, which is essentially providing healthcare and counselling. There are many different care pathways for kicking a heroin habit. Some are more successful than others, and they can be delivered in a variety of ways. Many are also used in tandem. The NTA boils the main methods down to five:

- counselling
- day centre
- detoxification
- prescribing
- residential

These can be delivered by and through a bewildering array of different services and agencies, which may vary slightly throughout the world depending on factors that include the policies of national and local government and the health authorities.

HEROIN TREATMENT

	NO OF ADMISSIONS	YEAR
Italy	121,000	1997
France	94,400	1997
Switzerland	19,000	1998
The Netherlands	19,000	1999
USA	216,900	1998

However, the first port of call for an addict wanting to quit a habit will probably be a call to their country's national drugs helpline, such as Narcotics Anonymous. This is likely to give confidential free advice 24 hours a day, and can put the heroin user in touch with other local agencies or groups. When someone is arrested they can also be routed towards drug agencies if they need treatment.

The family doctor or local hospital will also offer help to addicts trying to kick smack. In the UK, doctors make more referrals to specialist drug services than any other point of contact. The doctor can usually provide advice, sometimes prescribe substitute drugs, sometimes - although very rarely - prescribe heroin, often in tandem with a wide network of other specialist agencies and services.

There will also be a huge variety of different drug agencies, volunteer services, street agencies and community drug teams (which are multidisciplinary teams including counsellors, psychiatrists, social workers and advice services via the phone, drop-in centres or home visits). These confidential services will probably not simply confine themselves to the user, but will also involve the user's partner and friends.

Some may also have their own doctors, who may be able to prescribe drugs for detox or maintenance programmes and, if necessary, will steer the heroin user to other more appropriate services.

The quality of counselling and the qualifications of those providing it can vary, but these services are essentially designed to determine how serious users are about ridding themselves of their habit and to point them in the right direction to facilitate this. The street agencies and drug teams will also probably provide aftercare treatment, possibly combined with home visits or group therapy.

Syringe- and needle-exchange facilities are also available in many countries, including the UK, which pioneered their introduction in the 1980s. They provide clean works to heroin and other drug injectors, and are designed to stop the spread of HIV and other blood-borne viruses such as hepatitis C. Many are sited near drug-advice projects or hospitals, and some have their own confidential advice services and counsellors. Gary Sutton, heroin project adviser at Release, says he believes there is no proof that needle exchanges will increase the number of addicts on the streets, and that they have been 'absolutely central' in halting the spread of HIV in the UK. Outreach services will also attempt to bring the service to the user and may include a needle exchange and counselling service going into a heroin user's home.

The services of drug-dependency units are normally available for people who are heavy, long-term heroin users. Drug-dependency units are usually based within a hospital and provide another level of services on top of counselling, advice and information. These may include psychiatric treatment, advice on better syringe practice, needle exchange and home visits. Some may also offer a prescribing service and a detox service. Most can prescribe substitute drugs, such as methadone, in reducing script or maintenance programmes to stabilize the addict. Treatments can vary in different countries or even in different regions of a country, but will usually require a referral from a doctor or social worker. There is normally a waiting list.

Residential rehabilitation centres are also sometimes available for longer-term heroin users. Some offer detoxification on the premises, but most are only open to those who have already been through detox and are drug free. The addict will live in these rehabs for several months or more in a bid to kick their habit, although length of stay is often determined by costs, which are often very high. There are several types of programme available, but for heroin use the main ones tend to be based on the 'Minnesota model', which sees addicts work through a stepped programme, or a therapeutic approach, which includes intense therapy sessions.

FIRST PERSON
EDDIE COWLEY: DRUGS ARREST REFERRAL WORKER
'A lot of young drug users are in a terrible mess and it's
very disheartening. Sometimes I want to pack it all in
and become a dustman, but I carry on because I'd like to
think I can do some good. It's a result when anyone gets
off heroin but It's also a result to see someone clean and
healthy even If they're still using.

'When someone is arrested they are asked if they want
to see a drugs worker, irrespective of the offence. This is
a Home Office initiative aimed at tackling criminal
behaviour that is motivated by drugs. If the person in the
cells says "yes", I go into the police station to see them
and assess the problem, and refer them to drug agencies
if they need further treatment. Drug users' problems vary:
they could be jobless, homeless or maybe they have family
problems. The referral process can take six to eight months,
which is far too long.

'There are various options open to us within the criminal
justice system. The Drug Treatment and Testing Orders
(DTTOs) are mostly targeted at heroin users. People
committing crimes to feed their habit are put on a DTTO
and assigned a worker. They are put on a methadone
programme and tested regularly. The programme is designed
to keep them out of prison. The problem is that you have to
be arrested before you can get on to this type of programme.
Unless you've broken the law you can't get help.

'Methadone is prescribed in different ways. First, there is maintenance prescribing script in which users sign a contract and go on to a methadone programme. These tend to be long-term users. The problem with methadone is that it's very addictive. Drug users generally don't like it because it zonks them out completely. But at the moment methadone is all that's available for drug agencies.

'Second, there is the reduction prescribing script for people who want to come off heroin and methadone. The methadone dose is gradually reduced. Finally, there is the maintenance prescribing script with a view to detoxing. This is a residential detoxing programme and tends to be aimed at older people in their late twenties and thirties. Young people normally haven't finished their drugs career and aren't receptive to this particular remedy.

'I think the government genuinely does want to do something, but the money gets distributed in the wrong way. Services for people with drug problems are incredibly limited. The government concentrates too much on punitive measures and not rehabilitation and it isn't addressing the social causes of why people take heroin. Votes have a lot to do with it. The government wants to tackle crime figures rather than dealing with the underlying problems of heroin abuse.'

TYPES OF TREATMENT

Once a heroin addict has approached one of the main agencies or services for help, it will point them towards one or more of a whole range of treatment types and delivery models that are available. Again, different care and treatment types exist around the world, but the NTA's experience in the UK is typical.

In 2002, there were 120,000 people in drug treatment in the UK, approximately 100,000 of whom were heroin and opiate users. The NTA had set a target to have 200,000 entering treatment in 2008. However, treatments are really only successful when the heroin user wants to give up the drug and is not simply succumbing to pressure from a husband, wife or other family member or has been forced to reassess use because they are facing a prison term. There is no simple cure for heroin addiction and the user must decide for themselves that the drug is taking over - often ruining - their lives and they need help.

Treatment is also more effective if abuse is identified early. But in the early months and years of abuse many heroin users may not have been sucked into the debilitating side effects of the drug. It is only when their health suffers, they lose their jobs, homes and family or contract HIV that they look for help. Accessing people earlier also aids the efficacy of the resources ranged against drug addiction because younger people are more able to detox, whereas heroin users in their later twenties or early thirties often need methadone maintenance to first stabilize them, and that clogs the system.

Some evidence suggests that the method of administration may dictate how long a user waits before they ask for help. According to the US Substance Abuse and Mental Health Services Administration (SAMHSA) Treatment Episode Data Set 2001 those who inhaled heroin in 1998 sought treatment sooner than heroin injectors. On average, those snorting or smoking heroin sought treatment after six years. Injectors waited until they had been using a needle for about 11 years before seeking treatment.

More success is likely to result when agencies and services are combined or co-operate to offer the addict a multidisciplinary treatment. Thus, if a heroin user is trying to kick the drug with methadone at a residential clinic, then specialist drug workers should offer support when they returns home. Perhaps a support network of other past users will also operate in their area and they should be encouraged to attend.

In 2002 the NTA was seeking to introduce a Models of Care system, which would provide an integrated system for the heroin addict and highlight clearer care pathways. Someone would be responsible for determining the optimal route of treatment for an individual and also appointed to manage the whole 'journey' of an addict, through counselling, to detox or prescription.

According to Best and Witton, evidence also shows that the greatest gains are likely to result from longer stays in treatment. Other factors that could impact on the success of heroin treatment are whether the patient is allowed to take methadone home and the type of regime offered. They suggest that the treatment is likely to be more successful the more control the addict has.

METHADONE REDUCTION AND MAINTENANCE PROGRAMMES

Methadone, a synthetic opiate usually taken orally, is used in heroin replacement treatments. It induces less euphoria and blocks opioid receptors in the brain, avoiding withdrawal. It stabilizes the patient and reduces risks to their health in preparation for counselling, group work and reintegration into the community.

The effectiveness of treatment is largely dependent on the quality of the treatment and the commitment of the addict taking part. Properly prescribed methadone is not intoxicating or sedating, and its effects do not interfere with ordinary activities such as driving a car.

The medication can suppress narcotic withdrawal for 24 to 36 hours, and patients are able to perceive pain and have emotional reactions. Most important, methadone relieves the craving associated with heroin addiction; craving is a major reason for relapse. Methadone's effects last for about 24 hours – four to six times as long as those of heroin – so people in treatment need take it only once a day.

Methadone is used as a replacement for heroin in treatments aimed at either maintenance or gradual withdrawal. The reduction method is not particularly new and was suggested to help wean opium addicts off the drug in Thailand in the early 1800s. The modern treatment model was devised by the American physicians Professor Vincent Dole and Marie Nyswander in 1964. Methadone reduction treatment usually takes place in community settings and is designed to help the user withdraw or detoxify completely from opioid use. The aim is to gradually reduce the quantity prescribed until the user experiences no withdrawal symptoms and is drug free. The degree of reduction and length of time used to achieve abstinence can vary from a few weeks to many months, and motivation is the key to the success of these programmes.

Methadone maintenance treatment is a form of respite care, maintaining users by prescribing the drug to stabilize them. Methadone is medically safe even when used continuously for ten years or more. The theory behind the treatment is that methadone maintenance reduces some of the criminality associated with heroin and, because it is usually delivered in community settings, removes the risk of infection and enables those on the programme to live a normal life. In 2000 about 150,000 people were on methadone maintenance programmes in the USA. However, methadone does not automatically convert a heroin addict into a law-abiding citizen and must be backed up with aftercare, which can plug the abuser into a new, more fulfilling way of life.

Those opposed to methadone replacement argue that there is little evidence to suggest that criminal behaviour has been reduced or that those on programmes have been successful at finding work. Also, because it replaces one drug with another, it is not perceived as being a cure and, often, some methadone will find its way on to the black market.

Many heroin users approach methadone treatments, which have no aftercare or back up, as simply another drug supply – a pharmacological stop-gap – and when they can't find a ready supply of smack they will take the next available drug – methadone.

The US Substance Abuse and Mental Health Services Administration (SAMHSA) Treatment Episode Data Set 2001 also found that heroin inhalers were less likely than heroin injectors to receive methadone treatment. The use of methadone as part of treatment generally declined for both heroin injectors and inhalers from 1993 to 1998. The number of injectors on methadone fell from just over 60 per cent to less than 50 per cent and, for inhalers, from less than 50 per cent to 25 per cent in 1997.

Methadone remains the most widely used narcotic in treatment, but in recent years other synthetic drugs have been tested and in some countries, such as Australia and France, have been introduced into narcotic detoxification and maintenance therapy programmes as an alternative to methadone.

Buprenorphine was previously available for treating severe pain and its use in narcotic addiction is now spreading rapidly. A man-made narcotic, it is the least addictive powerful narcotic, and both an agonist and a blocker of the opioid nerve receptors. This means that it provides a moderate narcotic effect and blocks the craving for and effects of other narcotics.

Buprenorphine also produces a lower level of physical dependence, which means that patients who discontinue medication generally have fewer withdrawal symptoms than those who stop taking methadone. Because of these advantages, buprenorphine is also more appropriate for use in a wider variety of treatment settings.

Naloxone and naltrexone are medications that also block the effects of morphine, heroin and other opiates. As antagonists, they are especially useful as antidotes. Naltrexone has long-lasting effects, ranging from one to three days, depending on the dose. It blocks the pleasurable effects of heroin and is useful in treating some highly motivated individuals.

Naltrexone has also been found to be successful in preventing relapse by former opiate addicts released from prison.

OPIATE DETOXIFICATION

The primary objective of detoxification is to relieve withdrawal symptoms while patients adjust to a drug-free state. Not in itself a treatment for addiction, detoxification is a useful step only when it leads into long-term treatment that is either drug free (residential or out-patient) or uses medications as part of the treatment. The best-documented drug-free treatments are the therapeutic community residential programmes lasting at least three to six months.

However, it has also been known for some users to detox at home where the addict simply stops taking dope and goes through four or five days of painful withdrawal symptoms. The heroin user should cut down their dose to the minimum just prior to detox and make themselves comfortable, usually in bed. They should eat well and take cool showers and plenty of liquids. A family member or friend should also be enlisted to help out. However, even in a special detox unit there may be some suffering and often a high failure rate. There is also a high risk of OD if the detox fails and the heroin user returns to the streets for another score.

HEROIN PRESCRIBING

Heroin prescribing is available in several countries with more liberal attitudes towards heroin treatment, including the UK, The Netherlands, Australia, Switzerland and Spain. Before May 2002 there were only about 30 doctors in the UK who were still prescribing heroin to around 300 heroin users under licence (the government had stopped wholesale prescribing in 1968).

However, in early 2002 the NTA announced that it would examine the efficacy of reintroducing a wider system of prescribing heroin. Chief executive Paul Hayes said there were around 5 to 10 per cent of heroin users who didn't respond well to methadone and would probably do better on prescribed diamorphine. However, he conceded that the 'willingness of doctors is not great' and there were a number of issues that the treatment agency needed to address. 'There are cost implications because it is much more expensive. People have to use three times a day for the rest of their lives. And we've got to make sure it doesn't leak on to the market like it did in the 1960s and make sure we are not entrenching people in injecting behaviour. It is not an easy solution, but I'm pretty sure it's got a role to play,' he said.

Support for heroin prescribing also came from the UK police. In 2001 the Association of Chief Police Officers (ACPO) called for the mass prescription of heroin to addicts through specialist units in police stations, GPs' surgeries and hospitals. This would ensure that addicts had clean needles and health advice, and would keep contaminated needles off the street. ACPO president Sir David Phillips said at the time, 'The system has failed. We have an out-of-control drugs industry and it is time to try a new approach.' However, an ACPO spokesman said, 'It's not about legalizing heroin, but just the possibility of having heroin monitored and regulated from police stations.'

The Royal College of General Practitioners, however, voiced concerns about heroin prescribing in the UK in 2002. The college claimed it had a low therapeutic index and for a user who has lost their tolerance may be fatal. It also suggested it was too expensive, claiming that one year of methadone treatment cost £2,000 ($3,000) compared to around £10,000-15,000 ($14,500-22,000) for heroin.

Despite this, the UK drugs inquiry by the House of Commons Home Affairs Select Committee, chaired by Chris Mullin, recommended in May 2002 that a nationwide network of 'safe injecting areas' should be set up, with medical heroin prescribed by the National Health Service. Models of how heroin prescribing could be achieved were also being examined by the NTA.

Supervised consumption needs to be open at times that users can access it – usually late at night – and should also be secure so that drugs cannot be supplied to the illegal market. Often called 'shooting galleries', clinics where addicts can go for a health check, with provision for injecting and resuscitation equipment, have been piloted and used in Australia, Switzerland, Germany and other parts of Europe.

Switzerland's large-scale, long-term heroin maintenance experiment, in which a number of addicts were given regular doses of heroin under controlled conditions, has resulted in some dramatic results. Ueli

Minder of the Swiss Federal Office of Public Health said it has been accompanied by a fall in homelessness, a major reduction in illicit heroin and cocaine use, an improvement in the employment rate (in the treatment group) from 14 per cent to 32 per cent, and an eventual significant switch to other, more conventional treatments such as methadone maintenance and abstinence therapy.

Encouraged by five-year trials, the Dutch government also asked its parliament in March 2002 to endorse proposals to hand out heroin in combination with methadone to addicts who were 'beyond help'.

Sutton is in favour of shooting galleries because he says they reduce the visibility of addicts hanging around street corners and also the prevalence of discarded syringes. However, there are associated problems, he says. 'There are always people who don't want these things in their backyard. Also, how many addicts will go to a shooting gallery three times each day? But the alternative to shooting galleries is people's homes and you have to weigh the social consequences. What is the most damaging?'

Hayes said it would be unlikely that heroin prescribing would become the main form of medical treatment for heroin addiction. 'Methadone is likely to remain the most appropriate form of treatment for the majority of cases. There are, however, users who are not accessing treatment either because they have not responded well to the use of methadone, or because they refuse this form of treatment.'

He proposed that heroin prescribing could be used as a 'gateway treatment' to encourage users to enter other forms of treatment.

He also conceded that politics and the media play an important part in these treatments being made available. 'If there was a political move that this wasn't on, then it would be more difficult to achieve it,' he said. 'Certainly from our point of view we are being told to follow evidence. And if the evidence shows X works, then we want more X, whatever it is.'

BEHAVIOURAL THERAPIES

Although behavioural and pharmacological treatments can be extremely useful when employed alone, integrating both types of treatment will ultimately produce the most effective results. There are many effective behavioural treatments available for heroin addiction, which can include residential and out-patient approaches. An important task is to match the best treatment approach to the particular needs of the patient.

Several new behavioural therapies, such as contingency management therapy and cognitive-behavioural interventions, have been developed with some success for heroin addiction. Contingency management therapy uses a voucher-based system, where patients earn 'points' based on negative drug tests, which they can exchange for items that encourage healthy living.

The cognitive behavioural interventions are designed to help modify the patient's thinking, expectancies and behaviour and to increase skills in coping with various stress factors they encounter in the real world.

HEROIN MONEY

Like all commodities, heroin's market value goes up or down depending on a series of factors, such as the supply of opium, the size of the user market and its demand, the cost of smuggling and the scale of the profits taken by the crime organizations handling the drug. The National Criminal Intelligence Service estimated in 2002 that the mark-up on a kilo [2¼lb] of heroin was between £130,000 and £250,000 [$190,000 and $360,000], depending on the size of the drug-trafficking organization.

US research by the Office of National Drug Control Policy shows that heroin is getting cheaper. The 2001 study, 'The Price Of Illicit Drugs', shows that in the early 1980s users were spending up to $5 (£3.45) per milligram, but by the 2000s they were spending closer to $0.40 (28p) per milligram.

Heroin prices have fluctuated enormously since the beginning of the 1990s, partly due to law enforcement and the influence of governments in the main opium poppy regions. But one of the main catalysts has been the wars fought in Afghanistan. In the early 1990s, when the civil war in the country was at its height and opium production went unfettered, 1kg (2¼lb) of raw opium fetched around $40 (£28) on the open market.

With the Taliban gaining power, the price of Afghan opium – and therefore heroin – remained relatively stable. However, the regime's ban on poppy growing in 2000 sent the price of opium up to about $800 (£552) per kilo (2¼lb). The price crashed back to around $500 (£345) and stabilized in 2002 when the USA led attacks against the Taliban and Osama bin Laden in Afghanistan because opium farmers began planting again.

However, despite the massive fall in the production of opium it had little effect on prices in the UK and other European countries that are serviced by Afghan heroin. This was because producers had stockpiled supplies following a bumper crop in 1999 to keep supplies – and prices – level, although Luxembourg, Portugal, Sweden and the UK reported a slight decrease in 1999.

By 2002 there were signs that this was changing, with reports from users that the quality of heroin was dropping and the cost expected to increase. According to Addiction, the UK's biggest treatment charity, the cost of a gram in London, traditionally the most expensive market, was £60 ($87) in 2002. In other major UK cities, such as Birmingham, a gram could be bought for around £40 to £50 ($58 to $72).

Finding out how much the heroin market is actually worth in different countries is a difficult proposition, but in 2001 the UK Home Office attempted to put a value on it. The 'Sizing The UK Market For Illicit Drugs' report (see table overleaf), by the National Economic Research Associates for the Home Office, estimated that there were 270,000 regular heroin users in England and Wales, some 25,329 occasional users and several thousand in the prison population.

Assuming a regular heroin user, who on average used the drug on 24.6 days in the last 30, and spends about £28.80 ($42) per day on heroin, this equates to an annual drugs bill of £8,516 ($12,340). However, heroin users are often poly-drug users: the report cited that 53 per cent of regular heroin users also used crack cocaine and 24 per cent were regular cocaine users; almost 20 per cent of regular heroin users were regular users of both crack and cocaine; and the vast majority of regular crack users – 83 per cent – were also regular heroin users. The report therefore suggested they would spend a total of around £16,500 ($24,000) per year. It was, therefore, able to estimate that the total market for illicit drugs was £6.6 billion ($9.6 billion), with the heroin market easily the biggest part of that at £2.31 billion ($3.35 billion).

LEEDS COLLEGE OF BUILDING
LIBRARY

ILLICIT DRUG MARKET

TYPE OF HEROIN USER	NUMBER	SPEND
Regular	270,097	£2,299.9m
Occasional	25,329	£1.4m
Prison	3,331	£11.7m

TYPE OF DRUG	TOTAL VALUE OF MARKET
Heroin	£2,313m
Amphetamines	£257.7m
Cannabis	£1,577.9m
Cocaine	£352.8m
Crack	£1,817.4m
Ecstasy	£294.6m
Total value of illicit drug market	£6,613.5m

Note: £1 = $1.45 (approx)
Source: 'Sizing The UK Market For Illicit Drugs'

HEROIN LEGISLATION

Almost as quickly as drugs were introduced into society, laws were passed to limit their supply or – in more recent years – outlaw them totally. As long ago as 1729 the Chinese emperor Yung Cheng issued an edict prohibiting the smoking of opium and its sale, and in 1799 Kia King decreed poppy cultivation and its trade illegal.

In the West, the possession or supply of illicit drugs was largely not subject to prosecution until the middle of the 19th century, when the 1868 Pharmacy and Poisons Act was introduced following a spate of fatal opium overdoses in Britain. But it wasn't particularly effective as it was based on self-regulation and users could still get opiates over the counter at pharmacies.

In the USA, controls were also lax and inconsistent until 1875, when San Francisco passed a law to prohibit opium smoking. In 1890, in its earliest law enforcement legislation on narcotics, the US Congress imposed a tax on opium and morphine and, in 1906, followed up with the Pure Food and Drug Act. This required contents, labelling on medicines and other products containing opiates, and immediately cut the availability of opiates in drugstore powders and pills.

In 1909, the US Congress passed the first federal drug prohibition law – the Smoking Opium Exclusion Act – outlawing the importation and use of opium. Then, in 1910, the Chinese, who had fought two Opium Wars in 1839 and 1856 – with Britain in a bid to stop opium trafficking, finally persuaded the British government to dismantle the India-China opium trade and strictly enforce laws to restrict opium.

All modern global heroin legislation can essentially be traced back to 1909, when the first international Opium Commission was hosted by Shanghai. It focused primarily on opiate use in the Far East and countries with interests in that region and Persia were represented at the convention, which was chaired by Charles Henry Brent, the American Bishop of the Philippines, who became one of the most influential figures in combating drugs in the early part of the 20th century.

This conference laid the foundations for the International Opium Conference, held in The Hague in 1911. The British contingent, alarmed at the increased levels of smuggling in the Far East, proposed that the treaty should extend to the preparation and trade in morphine and cocaine. However, some countries – notably Germany – resisted this because they had huge pharmaceutical industries producing morphine-based drugs.

However, the conference did produce a treaty, the Opium Convention of 23 January 1912, which committed its 12 signatories to reducing opium and morphine abuse, and the drugs prepared from them, which included heroin. However, in reality, the Convention went no further than obliging the countries to take measures to control the trade in opium within their own legal systems.

A second conference, held in The Hague in 1913, was equally unsuccessful at ratifying the Convention and halting the production of heroin. Although the German pharmaceutical company Bayer ceased production of the drug in the same year, heroin supply was out of control, with many cocaine addicts switching to the cheaper alternative. It was only at a third conference in The Hague in 1914 that a protocol was signed allowing the Convention to take effect.

The USA gave substance to this Convention in 1914 with the Harrison Narcotics Act. This was the first comprehensive control of opiates, which curbed heroin and cocaine abuse and addiction by requiring doctors, physicians and chemists to register and pay a tax. Illegal possession of substances named in the Convention also led to a maximum fine of

$2000 (£1,380), five years' imprisonment or both. This also formalized the basis for the criminalization of the use of drugs in the USA for the next century.

The outbreak of World War I in 1914 interrupted further international law-making, though several European powers did move to tighten their border controls and domestic drug laws. For example, under a 1916 Spanish regulation, the sale of medicines was confined to prescriptions supplied at pharmacies, with stricter controls covering morphine.

The Netherlands also introduced an Opium Act in 1919 to outlaw opium-based drugs. However, by 1928, when possession was criminalized, the Dutch police often turned a blind eye and did not strictly enforce the country's drug laws.

In the UK, the government was worried about the uncontrolled supply of morphine and heroin throughout the armed forces and, in 1916, enacted Article 40(b) of the Defence of the Realm Act (DORA). This prohibited the supply of drugs, although not morphine, to army personnel and was later extended to encompass the whole country.

Following the end of the war and the signing of the Versailles peace treaty in 1919, the implementation of the 1912 international Opium Convention was made one of the conditions – Article 295 – of the peace deal. Responsibility for international narcotics legislation was put in the hands of the League of Nations and, in Britain, Article 295 became the Dangerous Drugs Act 1920.

This stipulated that only authorized bodies were allowed to manufacture or supply cocaine and opiates, such as morphine and heroin. Sales of drugs were logged and the Home Office began to regulate the import of opiates. Further legislation followed in 1923 with the Dangerous Drugs and Poisons Act, which amended the earlier Pharmacy Act.

In 1919, the League of Nations established the Social Questions and Opium Traffic Section and, by 1920, an Advisory Committee on Opium and other Dangerous Drugs was appointed. Britain, France (who in 1922 introduced a new law threatening ten years in prison for supply), The Netherlands, Japan, India, Portugal and China all had permanent representation on this committee.

The climate for opium and heroin legislation was also influencing a wider world. In 1925 a new narcotics law in Egypt outlawed trafficking in drugs and the growing of opium poppies, and a few years later introduced the Central Narcotics Intelligence Bureau, following a sharp rise in the number of heroin addicts in Cairo's slums.

Despite opposition from some prominent physicians, who believed that heroin offered relief to patients, drug supplies in the USA were further controlled in 1922 with the Jones-Miller Narcotic Drugs Import and Export Act. Heroin was eventually outlawed completely in 1924, with the introduction of the Porter Act. This made the manufacture and use of the drug in medicine illegal.

This set a pattern for much of the resulting prohibitionist

legislation governing heroin and opium supply over the next few decades, and demonstrated that the USA had not learned any lessons from the prohibition of alcohol: stamping out supply did not result in a downturn in demand. US narcotics agents, or narcs as they became known, from the Narcotics Division of the Prohibition Unit, were sent out to raid clinics and strangle the supply of legitimately produced medical supplies to addicts.

By 1923 the USA, which had not joined the League, began to attend Advisory Committee sessions and a further Opium Conference was opened in Geneva in November 1924. The first phase was directed at the issue of opium smoking, with a second phase, two months later, aimed at curbing opium derivatives, especially heroin.

The US was represented at the conference by chairman of the House Foreign Affairs Committee Stephen Porter, who proposed the world prohibition of heroin. However, most participants believed that, while illicit supplies remained uncontrolled, complete suppression was impossible, and rejected his blanket ban. The US delegation walked out.

Despite the walk-out, the Opium Conference, it passed a Convention that, in 1928, effectively put the control, manufacture, supply and sale of drugs in the hands of governments. Records on the levels of stocks of heroin and other drugs were ordered to be kept, and government departments took responsibility over their import and export.

The move had the effect of bringing into line the demand for legal morphine and heroin, required by legitimate hospitals and chemists, and the levels produced by licensed pharmaceutical companies. In the four years between 1928 and 1932, the global supply of 'legal' heroin fell by nearly 600 per cent.

In 1931, further conferences, which took place in Geneva and Bangkok, made efforts to suppress the illicit trade in narcotics and went further towards criminalizing the use of drugs by requiring all the Convention partners to introduce imprisonment for drug offenders. Restrictions were also placed on heroin, which at this point was being widely trafficked. However, with opium still being cultivated legally in the Far East, heroin use was not made a punishable offence at this stage.

A League of Nations convention for the Suppression of the Illicit Traffic in Dangerous Drugs followed in 1936, which made drug offences a crime punishable by extradition. A central office to supervise the prosecution of heroin and other drug traffickers was also established. Ironically, the USA refused to put its signature to the Convention because it did not include the trade in opium.

World War II also had the effect of mobilizing the legislators. Concerned that its troops would become junkies, the USA forced through an agreement to outlaw opium smoking in the Dutch East Indies in 1943, and the British also agreed to stop selling opium in its territories. This meant that just a few years after the war, opium smoking had been outlawed everywhere in the world apart from Thailand, which eventually got around to banning it in 1959.

The United Nations took over responsibility for heroin and other dangerous drugs from the League Advisory Committee on Opium and Dangerous Drugs in 1946. The UN established the Commission on Narcotic Drugs, made up of 40 member states, and this began preparations for a worldwide drugs policy.

In 1948, the World Health Organization (WHO) was drawn into helping to formulate this policy and, in 1949, attempted to instigate a worldwide ban on the manufacture and use of heroin. That view got a good hearing in the USA, where the Federal Bureau of Narcotics pushed for the compulsory imprisonment of drug users. The 1951 Boggs Bill also called for mandatory minimum sentences for opiate use and supply, ranging from between 2 and 5 years for a first offence and up to 20 years for third-time offenders.

The bill continued the momentum for more punitive overseas drug policies. The WHO recommended further drastic measures in 1953, when it called for all heroin production and imports to be wiped out. Then, in 1954, the UN pressed for the prohibition of the manufacture and trade in heroin unless it was destined for research or medical use. The British government, fearing that a blanket ban on legally produced heroin would create a massive market of illicitly produced heroin, did not seek to ban heroin manufacture.

However, it continued to restrict and control imports and exports of the drug. Also, in 1955, it did not renew licences for heroin production used in many cough remedies. Some other European countries, notably France and The Netherlands, followed suit.

The Boggs Bill was superseded by the 1956 Narcotic Control Act, which continued to pursue the USA's prohibitionist policies. Meanwhile, on the international stage, the UN introduced a single Convention on Narcotic Drugs in 1961. This replaced all previous Conventions and required participating governments to restrict the trade, production and possession of narcotics to scientific purposes. Any other activity was subject to punishment.

The Convention had four lists of substances, which were governed by a different regime of supervision. Also, on recommendations from the WHO, it could add new drugs to the lists if it could be shown that they presented a serious threat to public health or were part of illicit trafficking. Depending on the degree of misuse, substances could be transferred between lists and national legislation would then be adapted to reflect the changes.

A series of laws was also introduced in the UK during the 1960s to act on drug-abuse problems. These included the Drugs (Prevention of Misuse) Act 1964 and the Dangerous Drugs Act 1964, which ratified the 1961 New York convention, and imposed the requirement for safe keeping and recording of heroin and other drugs.

In 1967 the Misuse of Drugs Act made it necessary for a UK doctor to be issued with a Home Office licence to prescribe heroin to a patient, and also gave the authorities powers to rescind that right. The act also introduced stop-and-search powers on a national level, giving police more tools to investigate misuse and dealing if they suspected someone was in possession of a controlled drug.

In response to America's growing drug problem, Congress passed the Controlled Substances Act of the Comprehensive Drug Abuse Prevention and Control Act 1970. It replaced more than 50 pieces of drug legislation and came into effect on 1 May 1971.

This law established a single system of control for both narcotic and psychotropic drugs for the first time in US history. It also established five schedules to classify controlled substances according to how dangerous they are, their potential for abuse and addiction, and whether they possess legitimate medical value.

The Misuse of Drugs Bill 1971 became the template for the UK's modern drug laws, which aim to balance legislation to stop abuse without restricting the correct use of drugs to help manage disease and pain. The bill consolidated various pieces of legislation dating back to the early part of the 20th century and provided heavier sentences for trafficking and lighter ones for possession.

DRUG CATEGORIES

This bill outlined three categories (classes) of drugs according to their seriousness and awarded tariffs to punish offenders accordingly. Until 1985 it excluded barbiturates and still does not include other recreational drugs such as caffeine or amyl nitrate.

- Class A includes heroin, morphine and opium.
- Class B includes codeine and dihydrocodeine; Class B drugs can be classed as Class A if injected.
- The least severe, Class C, includes benzodiazepine, mild amphetamines and anabolic steroids.

Further efforts by the UK government to stop heroin traffickers from profiting from assets gained in the illegal supply of the drug came about with the Drug Trafficking Act of 1994. This holds that, if a defendant cannot provide a reasonable explanation as to the source of their assets, they can be seized.

Governments worldwide have not always followed logical and productive drug policies, primarily because drug use has been perceived as a criminal activity and not a treatable problem. However, as the new millennium dawned and it became clear that purely prohibitionist policies had failed to cut the supply of heroin or the number of addicts, the voices – and arguments – calling for the legalization of heroin became more powerful.

DECRIMINALIZATION

Governments have now started to examine policies that allow some decriminalization or legalization and would minimize the harm caused by drug abuse. The case for legalizing heroin begins with economists, who argue that any success in reducing the supply will raise the price of illegal drugs and cause more crime as addicts commit more burglaries or thefts to feed their habit. The resulting increase in profit margins earned by drug gangs will also spur them to greater efforts. The history of the drug trade is that supply always increases to meet demand.

In his respected 1994 book, *Winning The War On Drugs: To Legalize Or Not?*, Richard Stevenson, an economist at Liverpool University, wrote that all drugs should be legalized, marketed and regulated so that they can be controlled. He described a scenario where large companies produce, distribute and market heroin, and invest heavily in research to make drugs safer: 'I am prepared to argue that drugs should be as legal as beer. They could be available from chemists clearly labelled and unquestionably with a government health warning.'

Stevenson and others suggest that the benefits of legalization would be avoiding the criminal acts attributed to the cost of maintaining the supply of the drug. Policing and legal costs would fall, as would the size of the criminal sector and the attendant strain on the legal system, saving the country millions. Legalization would pass heroin production, supply and profits from criminals to respectable tax-paying businessmen, and the government could earn millions. It is also likely that the price of heroin would fall by removing the legislation controlling it, which would leave the addict more money for food, clothing and to look after their health needs.

This view has drawn wide – and sometimes surprising – support from a number of quarters, which argue that governments cannot control the supply and quality of drugs until they are in charge of things, and that treatment, rather than jail sentences, should be available for drug abusers.

Fulton Gillespie, parent of a heroin victim and a witness to the 2002 UK drugs inquiry by Chris Mullin's Home Affairs Select Committee argues that it is futile to try and stop young people taking drugs. He suggests that society has a greater responsibility to make drug taking safe. 'Those who believe legalization will make more hard drugs available to more young people overlook the fact that drugs of all kinds are more available to more young people now than ever, even with prohibition in force. There is not a whit of evidence to support the idea that there is some massive reservoir of disaffected youth about to rush out and die. There are more pushers out there than chemists' shops, so those who want to use hard drugs are using them now and will continue to use them, come what may,' he said.

In 2001, a call for a debate about legalization also came from certain sectors of the police. North Wales chief constable Richard Brunstrom published *The Drugs Debate: Time For Change?* in which he conceded that the war against the illegal drugs trade has failed, and also said that the attempt to control drugs' availability and supply had not worked. 'Proscription is not working,' he wrote. 'Drugs are ever more freely available... There is no logic to the proscription list – alcohol and tobacco are our biggest killers.' His views were supported by former Gwent police chief constable Francis Wilkinson, who called for heroin to be legalized. He added, 'The current drug laws make the situation worse and any form of legalization would be preferable.'

In 2002 former UK government cabinet minister Mo Mowlam also argued that strict prohibition had not worked and called for the legalization of all drugs, including heroin. Mowlam said that the money raised from taxing drugs could be used for treatment. 'If the kids get hold of it because it's a high, they will get hold of it. Why not regulate it, take the tax from it, and deal with addiction?' she asked.

UK HEROIN OFFENCES
POSSESSION
A person has heroin under their control; but supplying a person who is legally entitled to have the drug is not an offence. Possession of heroin in the UK will result in six months' imprisonment, a £5,000 ($7,570) fine, or both, in

a magistrates' court. In a crown court, penalties are more serious, at seven years, an unlimited fine or both.

POSSESSION WITH INTENT TO SUPPLY

The amount of heroin is not always relevant and even giving a small bag to a friend for safe keeping falls under this charge. If the friend returns the bag, they will also be found guilty of supply. If the amount seized in a person's possession appears to be more than for personal use that might also be used as evidence of intent. Evidence of scales, cutting equipment and bags, used in the wholesale supply of heroin, will also be used by the prosecution. In a magistrates' court, possession of heroin with intent to supply could earn six months' jail, a £5,000 ($7,550) fine or both. In the crown court, the person could be sentenced to life or be required to pay an unlimited fine.

USE OF PREMISES

If a householder allows their premises to be used for the consumption of heroin, then they are liable to between six months' and 14 years' imprisonment and a fine of £5,000 ($7,550) or more.

The Misuse of Drugs Act regulations divide controlled drugs into five schedules, which list drugs according to who may lawfully produce, trade and handle them:

- drugs in Schedule 1 include heroin and are the most stringently controlled because they can only be supplied

or possessed with a Home Office licence;
- drugs in Schedules 2 to 4 are available for medical use, but are normally controlled by a prescription: temazepam, for example, is listed under Schedule 4 and can be possessed if it has been prescribed for medical use;
- at the other end of the scale, Schedule 5 drugs can be sold over the counter at chemists.

LEGISLATION AROUND THE WORLD

AUSTRALIA
Heroin production and importation were prohibited in 1953 by Commonwealth legislation.

AUSTRIA
The Narcotics Law 1951 originally allowed consumption of narcotics. But in 1985 lighter legislation was introduced and the Methadone Act 1987 now regulates methadone substitution.

BELGIUM
The Ministry of Interior, Ministry of Justice and Ministry of Health divide up crime prevention, legal and criminal areas, and drug-prescription monitoring. Providing syringes for the illegal consumption of drugs is a crime.

BULGARIA
Several laws were passed in the early 1970s to restrict and

prohibit drug trafficking and consumption. Anyone testing HIV positive is obliged to report for a medical.

CZECH REPUBLIC
Restrictive drug laws were introduced after the Velvet Revolution in 1989, although heroin is still cheaper here than in western Europe.

DENMARK
Danish law makes no distinction between hard and soft drugs, and needles are sold from vending machines in Copenhagen and other cities.

FINLAND
The Care of Substance Abusers Act 1985 enforces the use of compulsory treatment where applicable. Possession and use of drugs is illegal.

FRANCE
No distinction between hard and soft drugs. Severe penalties for trafficking and most prosecutions are for possession, not use.

GERMANY
Germany's Drug Act has three levels of categories for narcotics: completely forbidden (which includes heroin); strictly regulated and not acceptable to prescribe; and

strictly regulated, but can be prescribed medically.

IRELAND
Possession for personal use is punishable with up to seven years for hard drugs, and a fine and up to three years for soft drugs.

ITALY
An action plan to consolidate the country's fight against drugs came into force in 1990 with a law on drug dependence.

LATVIA
No distinction between hard and soft drugs.

LITHUANIA
No distinction between hard and soft drugs. Drug use could result in a prison sentence of between 15 days and 24 months, depending on number of convictions. Trafficking punishable with prison terms of between 6 and 15 years.

LUXEMBOURG
Heroin users can be compelled to undergo compulsory treatment.

THE NETHERLANDS
No police action to detect offences involving the possession

of drugs for personal use. No legal restrictions on the distribution of methadone or the sale of syringes.

NORWAY

Crimes against the country's Drugs Act are liable to heavy fines, with a maximum prison sentence of 21 years. A tip-off telephone line was introduced in 1990 to enable the public to inform on heroin or other drug dealers.

POLAND

Poland's Drug Abuse Prevention Act 1985 includes obligatory treatment for users under the age of 18.

PORTUGAL

Heroin traffickers and users face prison sentences. Syringes are available free under a needle-exchange programme.

ROMANIA

Drug laws were passed in 1969 and 1979 to regulate the production, possession and circulation of narcotics.

RUSSIA

In 1998, the liberal Federal Law on Drugs and Psychotropic Substances, which made a distinction between the dealer and consumer of heroin, was replaced by a new Federal Law. An amount of heroin exceeding 0.005g is now punishable by a prison sentence of up to 15 years.

SPAIN
Distinguishes between hard drugs and soft drugs. The sale of syringes is permitted.

SWEDEN
Generally, drug policy is repressive and restrictive, and the maximum sentence for a drugs-related offence is 14 years.

UK
The principal legislation is the Misuse of Drugs Act 1971, which divided drugs into three categories (Class A, Class B and Class C) according to their degree of harmfulness. Heroin is a Class A drug.

UKRAINE
Still governed by tough laws from the Soviet regime. Syringes are not widely available.

HEROIN CRIME
As soon as drug laws were introduced, handling heroin became a crime, and criminal gangs grew to profit from it. Like the alcohol-banning Volstead Act 1919 in the USA, which heralded a decade of Prohibition and created criminal gangs willing to supply bootlegged booze, the introduction of tougher drug legislation in the USA and Europe ledinexorably to control of the heroin business by organized crime.

DRUG RUNNING

The American smugglers John Cushing and John Jacob Astor had already made vast profits from shipping Turkish opium to Canton in the 18th century after poppy cultivation in China had been banned. But the new drug laws of the early 1920s were seen as a new opportunity for a new breed of gangster: the drug runner.

One of the first and biggest American drug traffickers was Arnold Rothstein, who had made a fortune from gambling, illegal liquor and Prohibition dens such as the notorious Cotton Club. Almost as soon as the Jones-Miller Narcotic Drugs Import and Export Act 1922 and the Porter Acts were in place, Rothstein's and gangs run by others were shipping opiates and cocaine back to the USA from Europe.

The drugs were cut and distributed stateside and the criminals' success was illustrated by a sixfold increase in the amount of narcotics seized by US Customs in just one year, from 1925 to 1926. Organized crime and the smuggling of heroin exploded alongside the new prohibitionist policies, sponsored by the USA and followed by Europe, during the 1920s.

The earliest drug racketeers included the Frenchman Henry de Monfreid in Europe and Africa and, in the USA, the Jewish gangster Meyer Lansky, the mobster Lucky Luciano, a hired hand of Rothstein who had been arrested in 1916 for dealing in heroin, and Jack 'Legs' Diamond, another Rothstein employee suspected of killing a New York heroin courier in 1928.

They set the rules, ruthlessly enforced them and became the prototypes for the cold-blooded, but hugely profitable Turkish, French and Corsican heroin drug gangs that emerged in the 1970s and were followed by the Colombians and Mexicans a decade later.

The injured of World War I increased the number of morphine – and later heroin – addicts and as demand for drugs rose, illegal supplies also increased. Initially illicit heroin found its way on to the illegal drug market following break-ins at pharmaceutical manufacturers. However, opiates were also supplied from legitimate drug companies with the Allied occupying forces in Germany and across Europe, providing well-trained traffickers of heroin and morphine.

The British banned Hoffmann-La Roche's products throughout its empire in 1925, although lifted the control a year later after the Swiss group introduced a system of controls on exports. But leaks of heroin, which found their way on to the illicit market, came from other European drug companies, and secret illicit laboratories were also set up to take over the supply of opiates and heroin.

In Britain, Assistant Under Secretary of State, Sir Malcolm Delevingne, urged the elimination of traffickers as the only way to cut out heroin and other drug users. Similarly, the USA was taking steps to stop the international traffickers. An international network was set up in 1930 to catch the gangs, with US agents spread through Europe and working with British and French drug-enforcement units.

The problem with breaking the gangs was that the supply and production of opium had increased. India had always been an important producer of opium, but Persia became an increasingly important exporter of poppies to the Far East, Russia and Europe in the 1920s. The opium was turned into heroin in illegal labs set up in Japan and throughout Asia.

Opium was also available in China and opium gangs quickly sprang up to supply illicit heroin in this region and Hong Kong, which became a magnet for organized crime gangs in the 1930s. In the early years of heroin manufacture and trafficking, the Balkans also became an important crime centre. Bulgaria, Serbia and Turkey all produced opium poppies, and European and Japanese traffickers set up heroin factories in cities such as Constantinople.

By 1930 poppy growing was being phased out in India, and Turkey had assumed the mantle of the world's major heroin producer. Istanbul became a magnet for French and Japanese illegal producers and traffickers, and by the mid-1930s it was estimated that over 72,000kg (65 tonnes/tons) of heroin was being manufactured in the city.

France also had its problem with illicit heroin manufacturers, who bought opium in Turkey, processed it into heroin and supplied the drug to the USA and the Far East. And in Bulgaria, which was party to the Geneva limitation agreements, opium-poppy cultivation multiplied in the early part of the 19th century, with illicit heroin factories established in Sofia.

In Japan, mercenaries were used throughout the 1920s and 1930s to help traffic the illicit heroin that Japanese pharmaceutical companies were manufacturing, for supply mainly to China. By the mid-1930s the Japanese army gave protection to drug traffickers in China, and the government actually encouraged opium growing and the supply of narcotics like heroin to overseas countries as part of its foreign policy to help colonize parts of the Far East. By the start of World War II, Japan was the world's biggest supplier of heroin.

Opium and heroin traffickers also emerged in Russia, where Manchuria became an important centre for shipping illicit drugs. In Germany and Austria, pharmaceutical companies were also manufacturing more morphine-based drugs than domestic supply warranted and much of it found its way into criminal hands. US trafficker Arnold Rothstein often bought directly from Berlin factories, although the rise of Hitler and the Nazi Party clamped down on leakages.

In the same way as the Opium Exclusion Act 1909 had caused an increase in the illegal trade in heroin, a 1925 crackdown on opiates in Egypt also helped increase the use and supply of heroin. Switzerland was also a notorious supplier of morphine and heroin, which was sometimes smuggled inside clocks or boxes of chocolates, or disguised as less harmful drugs.

Tough drug laws also encouraged drug trafficking in Latin America in the mid-1920s. Chile, Argentina, Peru and Honduras all became major centres for gangsters dealing in opium, morphine and heroin. Some couriers employed fake certificates to get around the limitations imposed by the League of Nations and also used the practice of diplomatic immunity to bypass customs.

Illegal heroin labs had first been discovered near Marseille in 1937. These labs were run by the legendary Corsican gang leader Paul Carbone. For years the French underworld had been involved in the manufacturing and trafficking of illegal heroin abroad, primarily to the USA. Marseille's convenience and the frequent arrival of ships from opium-producing countries made it easy to smuggle the morphine base, but the port's prominence as a major centre for heroin export was sealed in the late 1940s when the US Central Intelligence Agency (CIA) armed and funded Corsican gangs in their opposition to French communists.

THE FRENCH CONNECTION

Corsican gangs took control of the French port's illegal trade in opium and heroin and, by the early 1950s, it was a major link between the Sicilian Mafia and US heroin users: this was the 'French Connection'. This new phase in the development of heroin crime came when the USA unwittingly helped traffickers by linking them to the Mafia in Sicily.

In 1946, America deported hundreds of gangsters, including Lucky Luciano, whose experience and expertise in the heroin trade interested Mafia bosses in Palermo. The Mafia began buying opium. They mostly bought from Turkey, whose farmers were licensed to grow opium poppies for sale to legal drug companies, but sold their excess to the underworld market. The Mafia also opened heroin labs in Marseilles and Sicily to process the heroin and then smuggle the drug to US and Canadian cities.

The first significant post-World War II seizure was made in New York in 1947, when 3kg (7lb) of heroin were seized from a Corsican seaman disembarking from a vessel that had just arrived from France. In 1949, more than 23kg (50lb) of opium and heroin were seized on the French ship *Batista*, but the first major French Connection case occurred in 1960 when an informant told a drug agent in Lebanon that Mauricio Rosal, the Guatemalan Ambassador to Belgium, The Netherlands and Luxembourg, was smuggling morphine base from Beirut to Marseilles. In one year alone, Rosal had used his diplomatic status to smuggle about 200kg (440lb) of smack.

The French traffickers continued to exploit the demand for their product and by 1969 were shipping to the US between 80 to 90 per cent - around ten tonnes of heroin - of all its heroin supply. The heroin they supplied was also very good, approximately 85 per cent pure. The French Connection continued into the 1970s, but was finally cut following a 1971 political coup in Turkey, which saw a new regime willing to ban opium growing in return for US aid.

NEW ROUTES

With the fall of the French Connection new supplies were needed to satisfy the USA market, and Mexico helped fill the gap, with the rise of Latin smugglers shipping across the Texan and Californian borders. At about the same time the Mafia was being joined by Cuban gangs in importing heroin into the USA. Cubans had begun settling in Florida following the disastrous 1961 Bay of Pigs invasion, but further criminal immigrants arrived over the next two decades, including thousands of criminals deported by Fidel Castro.

Further illegal heroin supplies followed another disastrous US foreign policy intervention. The CIA began to give assistance to the Chinese Nationalists in the 1950s. Unfortunately, they trafficked in opium. In the following decade, the CIA pumped arms into Laos near the border with Vietnam to support Hmong tribesmen in resisting communism. Again, the anti-communists' main source of funding was the opium poppy and these heroin warlords expanded opium production by pledging that the money raised would help fight communism. The CIA was even complicit in helping move the opium to labs in the Golden Triangle (Myanmar, Laos and Thailand), and heroin was shipped to Vietnam and other countries in the region.

During the Vietnam War, some 10 per cent of US soldiers

were thought to be heroin users and until the US withdrawal from Vietnam in 1973, it is thought that about one-third of the illicit heroin that washed up on the streets of US cities came from the Golden Triangle labs the CIA had helped set up.

In 1979, US President Jimmy Carter began helping the Mojaheddin guerrillas in resisting the Soviet occupation of Afghanistan. However, like the tribesmen in Laos, the Afghan fighters grew and sold opium poppies to help finance their war. By 1980, over half of the heroin flooding into the USA was from Afghanistan and the country remains the world's largest illicit opium producer, with a proliferation of heroin factories in Pakistan.

The war in Kosovo in 1999 also inadvertently led to Europe being flooded with smack. Following the NATO bombing campaign, which forced Serbian forces out of the ethnic Albanian province, the region became a centre for smugglers unfettered by law enforcement. Agencies estimated that some 40 per cent of the heroin sold in Europe and North America was flowing through the province in 2000, with the traffickers handling up to five tonnes of heroin each month compared to around two tonnes before the conflict.

The links between heroin and crime were made startlingly clear in 2001 when UK Home Office research showed that 29 per cent of all arrestees tested positive for opiates or cocaine, and that about one-third of the proceeds of acquisitive crime went back towards buying heroin or crack.

Partly as a result of these findings, the UK shifted its emphasis on tackling criminals to targeting the profits they make through heroin. Marking the introduction into Parliament of the Proceeds of Crime Bill, which was designed to dismantle and disrupt criminal gangs, Home Office minister Bob Ainsworth said, 'Criminals should not be allowed to profit from their crime. Crime barons make their money off the back of local communities' misery. They cash in on the illegal drug markets, burglary and muggings that plague innocent people's lives.'

By 2002 the UK's law-enforcement agencies also admitted that they had adopted the wrong strategy – of focusing resources on individuals and seizing heroin shipments – for drug crimes. It was also reported that they had accepted they did not know about 60 per cent of the drug trade.

In a radical shift, UK police and customs accepted that their future approach would concentrate on choking off the profits of traffickers: chasing profits, not powder. One tactic was to mount covert surveillance on suspected bureau de change outlets, which are used by drug gangs to launder money.

HEROIN TRAFFICKING METHODS
THE SEEDS OF SMUGGLING
Heroin's journey to the streets of New York, London or Paris begins with the planting of the opium poppy. Around three

months after the poppy seeds have been planted, the milky opium sap is harvested, and the dark brown gum shaped into bricks or cakes and wrapped in plastic.

These are sold by the farmer to a dealer, who will probably have a morphine-refining plant – nothing more elaborate than a few drums and a stove in a rudimentary lab – close by. The opium brick will be mixed with lime in boiling water until a band of morphine forms on the surface and can be drawn off; it is then reheated with ammonia, filtered, and boiled again until reduced to a brown paste.

The morphine base, with the consistency of modelling clay, will be poured into moulds and dried in the sun ready for further processing into heroin. This may take place in another illicit lab, albeit a more sophisticated one.

When the heroin emerges from these labs it enters a complex chain of distribution. Large dealers will usually deal in shipments of anything up to several hundred kilos, which will then be divided into smaller packages of between 1kg (2¼lb) and 10kg (22lb) for sale to street gangs. These will be split further into bags of a gram or less for sale to users. The number of street dealers in a given area can vary enormously and will depend on the number of heroin users present, police activity and even the area's historical status as a drug-dealing centre. King's Cross in London and the East Village in New York, for example, have reputations as places to cop.

SUPPLYING DEMAND

The more the law-enforcement measures are upgraded, the more complicated the drug traffickers' modus operandi becomes. In the course of the struggle against drug trafficking, anti-drug control forces have been faced with a wide spectrum of concealment methods.

Typically, different drug gangs will control cultivation and production levels, and regulate prices. At the wholesale level, however, the trafficking process becomes more diversified and can involve a number of different smuggling groups and brokers. Brokers will often have close connections with several rival producers, and heroin traffickers form limited partnerships with different groups to ensure business flexibility, continual supply and a measure of protection from the law.

CONCEALMENT METHODS

Heroin moves from the region of source and production to the consuming markets by a variety of methods, usually involving either air, sea or land, or a combination of these. Heroin smugglers have been forced to be more creative because trafficking laws are increasingly stringent, and police and customs officials are devising new ways to detect drugs.

It is a challenge traffickers are rising to. New techniques are seemingly limited only by a trafficker's imagination and are being helped by new technology. However, invariably the most effective methods are the simplest. Air and sea remain the principal methods of transporting large amounts of Southeast Asian, Afghan and South American heroin to markets such as the USA and Europe. The high volume of commercial air and maritime traffic provides a natural camouflage for heroin concealed in containers, and multiple port transfers help obscure the origin of the illicit cargo.

COURIERS AND MULES

Trafficking groups also use couriers, or 'mules', to smuggle small amounts of heroin, usually up to 2kg (4½lb), on commercial flights or through border crossings in private cars or on foot. The mules conceal the heroin in their luggage, body cavities or stomachs by drug swallowing. This is one of the commonest and most dangerous methods of concealment; the narcotics are packed in small multilayered plastic bags. Despite the danger of these being torn up in the stomach, the mules are paid very little.

Other, more imaginative and bizarre ways of smuggling heroin through customs are always being tested and, in February 2002, one mule flying into a Florida airport was stopped after it was discovered that a Colombian laundry had starched all his shirts and jeans using over two pounds of heroin. Customs inspectors stopped the mule after noticing the unusually stiff clothes that smelled of vinegar and left a trail of white powder. Another border patrol in

Texas uncovered $5 million (£3.5 million) worth of narcotics stuffed inside the body parts – legs, arms and intestines – of a stolen corpse. The traffickers used the body to disguise the scent of the drugs from sniffer dogs.

Criminal groups supplying the USA from South America or from Mexico often use the land route through the southwest border with Texas. Illegal immigrants and migrant workers smuggle between 1kg (2½lb) and 3kg (6½lb) loads, but larger amounts are delivered by truck.

Mexican heroin-distribution networks in the United States are managed almost entirely by criminal organizations operating from Mexico and by Mexican-American criminal gangs that are in charge of the street-level distribution of heroin. Groups from the Dominican Republic have also played a significant role in retail-level heroin distribution using bases in east-coast cities, including New York, Boston, and Philadelphia.

In Afghanistan and neighbouring countries like Pakistan and Iran, less sophisticated, but by no means less successful, modes of heroin transportation are used. These can include jeep, motorbike or even camel caravans, which can carry up to seven tonnes (tons) of narcotics. The advantage of these methods is that there is no need for smugglers to accompany the caravan, which can be controlled by traffickers operating from remote mountainous areas.

Trafficking organizations employ drug distribution network and creative marketing techniques to expand the heroin market in the country they are supplying. There have been instances of some gangs providing free samples of heroin to traditional cocaine or other drug buyers in order to attract new custom.

During the smuggling process the weight and the bulk of the drug is kept to a minimum and heroin is handled in as highly concentrated a state as possible, often with a purity exceeding 90 per cent. Before sale, it is diluted several times. The substances used for adulteration vary considerably, but include fenacetine and methaqualone, which have intoxicating properties themselves.

Southeast Asian heroin traffickers typically deal in 700g (25oz) units, in contrast with South American, Mexican and Southwest Asian heroin traffickers, who traffic in kilogram quantities. When produced in refineries in Southeast Asia, heroin is usually packaged in half-unit blocks (350g [12oz] per block) of compressed powder. These rectangular blocks are 2.5cm (1in) thick and measure 13 by 10cm (5 by 4in).

CONTAINERIZED CARGO

Because of the huge volume of worldwide commercial trade and the necessity of containerized cargo, heroin traffickers continue to employ commercial containerized cargo on aircraft and merchant ships as a successful smuggling method.

For example, heroin processed in the Golden Triangle (Myanmar, Laos and Thailand) is smuggled overland to Myanmar, China, Thailand, Malaysia and Vietnam for transhipment by air or sea within containerized cargo through Taiwan, Hong Kong, Singapore, Japan and Korea. From these transit countries, the heroin is shipped to consumer markets in Europe, Australia, Canada and the USA.

Many characteristics are common among containerized-smuggling heroin trafficking gangs. They include renting or buying import/export companies or warehouses within the source and transit countries, such as Thailand and the USA, for the sole purpose of smuggling and storing drugs. Heroin traffickers will frequently change the names of these 'front companies', but they sometimes maintain the same addresses and will remain as long as the companies have not themselves been compromised.

Typically, one entire 8m (20ft) or 16m (40ft) container is leased and filled with a cheap range of goods. Popular lines for heroin smugglers are plastic bags, soy sauce, T-shirts and chopsticks; however, gangs often use seafood and other perishables as a way of discouraging customs inspection.

Usually the commodity is packed in cardboard cartons of uniform size and weight, and stacked on pallets. The cartons containing the heroin are placed deep within the container. There may be only one pallet that contains all the cartons of heroin, or single cartons of heroin may be placed among the individual cartons of the commodity, but as a rule fewer than ten cartons of heroin will be concealed within around 1,000 cartons of the commercial cargo.

Concealment methods in the cartons also vary. For example, the heroin may be placed in cans that are weighted the same as the canned commodities or it may be formed into the shape of the items in the cartons. Traffickers will also add weights in an attempt to minimize differences between those packs containing heroin and those not.

Drug-laden cartons will also be marked or numbered to distinguish them from the legitimate commercial cargo cartons. For example, a woman's image was stamped on one shipment, and the boxes containing the heroin were identified by shading in one of the woman's eyes.

Containers will also be insured for up to ten times more than the actual value of the commercial cargo and, in many cases, heroin shipments will transit a secondary port prior to shipment to the final destination to put officials off the trail. For example, heroin produced within the Golden Triangle may be shipped to secondary ports in Taiwan, China, Hong Kong, Malaysia, Singapore, Tokyo or South Korea. A new bill of lading will be issued to indicate that the cargo originated somewhere other than the Golden Triangle.

HI-TECH SMUGGLING

New technologies are also increasingly being used by the heroin smuggler. In its 2001 Annual Report, the International Narcotics Control Board (INCB) highlighted its concerns about the misuse of new technologies in international drug control. The board said that drug-trafficking groups utilize new technologies, such as the Internet and electronic pocket organizers that can store contact- and bank-account details, sales records and coordinates for landing strips, to improve the efficiency of heroin's delivery and distribution. Drug traffickers were also using encrypted messages in computers to conceal information about drug shipments, and to protect themselves and their illicit operations from investigation by drug law enforcement agencies.

WHAT HEROIN CRIME COSTS

It costs money to fight, but there are a number of other links between heroin and crime. Addicts often resort to burglary, shoplifting, fraud or other theft to support their habit. This contributes a large share of costs to a country through the damage or loss of property, the cost of replacing it and insurance.

Some people will be caught in possession of, or supplying, illegal heroin. This will add to law enforcement, police and court time and costs.

Further crimes, ranging from manslaughter to driving offences, may also be committed while under the influence of heroin. Violence between rival gangs of heroin dealers, or between a dealer and a dependent user, will also count towards the crime figures and costs.

Finding out how much heroin crime costs is a very complex process, however, and little or no consensus has been reached. In the USA, annual economic costs related to drug abuse were estimated to be $110 billion (£76 billion) a year, or 1.5 per cent of GDP in the mid-1990s (UN drug report, 2000), but the many estimates that have attempted to find out the 'cost-of-crime' element have pitched figures anywhere between $1 and $3 billion (£0.7 billion and £2 billion).

Similarly, in the UK, attempts have been made to accurately assess the size of the illegal market in heroin and the cost of drug-related crime, specifically, how much heroin contributes to the bottom line of the UK bill.

UK researchers have suggested that there are between 130,000 and 200,000 problematic drug users in the UK, committing theft and other crimes to support habits costing each of them up to £30,000 ($43,500) annually. However, since stolen goods only fetch about one-third of their value, the total cost of stolen goods could be up to £2.5 billion ($3.6 billion) each year.

Further research about the cost of heroin abuse on society was revealed in 2002 when research by the University of York was presented by Bob Ainsworth, Parliamentary Under Secretary of State at the UK's Home Office with responsibility for anti-drugs co-ordination and organized crime. It showed that drug abuse in England and Wales costs society up to £18.8 billion ($27.2 billion) a year, with hardcore heroin and crack cocaine addicts responsible for some 99 per cent of that bill (it estimated that there were 281,125 heroin or cocaine users whose 'habits were no longer under control' and that they are each costing the state around £30,000 [$43,500] a year, or £600 [$870] each week).

Furthermore, the research stated that the UK's National Health Service spent £235 million ($341 million) on doctor services, accident and emergency admissions, and other treatment linked to drug abuse. When these health-service costs are added to the criminal justice system and the welfare state, costs rise to between £3.7 billion and £6.8 billion ($5.4 billion and $9.9 billion). However, with the addition of social costs the bill rises to between £10.9 billion and £18.8 billion ($15.8 billion and $27.2 billion).

ADDITIONAL INFO

SUMMARY

For the past few decades, the world has been fighting a war on heroin, but with many countries using only the limited weapons of legislation and punishment, few have managed to isolate the enemy, let alone slay it. Most have tried to reduce the user population, only to see it rise. They have tried to strangle the supply, only to see it increase and heroin prices fall. And they have tried to inflict casualties on crime gangs that profit from heroin, only to see them proliferate and get richer.

It seems that almost every effort to wipe heroin from the face of the planet has failed. The policy makers in many countries are now at an important crossroads and face a tough question: will they persist in fighting a principled but ultimately ineffectual campaign against heroin, or do they accept that the war cannot be won and opt for living with the drug while putting in place systems and treatment to minimise its effects on users and society?

It appears that most westernized countries are now acknowledging the fact that, if there is one single lesson

LEEDS COLLEGE
LIBRARY

to be learned from the experience of the last 30 years, it is that policies based on enforcement are destined not to succeed. The best that the world's lawmakers can claim to have done is to partly stem heroin's spread. At worst, they have simply created new problems of organised crime. Therefore, the reduction of harm rather than retribution seems to offer a more effective way of dealing with the problem.

As Chris Mullin, chairman of the UK's Home Affairs Select Committee, which in May 2002 published one of the most far-reaching reports on drugs in Britain, said, 'We have to face the fact that, whether we like it or not, large numbers of young people take drugs. As far as users are concerned, our priorities should be realistic education, readily available treatment, and harm reduction. Above all, we have to focus on that relatively small minority of drug users who are making a misery of their own lives and those of others.'

With this in mind, it appears that more countries are now willing to pick up and use new tools to combat heroin and its abuse, and some have signalled their intention to follow the lead set by countries such as Australia, The Netherlands and Switzerland, who have adopted progressive drug measures and taken a more enlightened approach to the ways in which they tackle the problem of heroin. In due course, these new ways of reaching and treating the heroin addicts who cause most damage to themselves and others will include looking at the efficacy of prescribing heroin – which would undercut the illegal heroin market and drug-related crime – and the provision of 'shooting galleries' – safe-injecting rooms – which would take the most chronic addicts off the street.

These and other new methods will also be tried and tested – and, in some instances, discarded – over the next decade as evidence is gathered to back up their use. However, in the long term, as costs are met and political and social resistance is overcome, it is likely that more harm-reduction treatments will move automatically from the pilot stage to being nationally or universally adopted. In some countries, use of these methods may even require changes in law to allow pharmacists to supply drug users with relevant paraphernalia, such as swabs, citric acid and needles, in order to reduce the risks of heroin use.

At the same time, the future success of moves to deal with heroin lies in better education, with a view to stopping users from taking up heroin in the first place. Drugs are increasingly part of most young people's lives and it's essential that the world's governments get balanced, accurate information about them across to their young. However, the area is under-resourced and there is still a huge and unresolved debate over the effectiveness of many of the drug campaigns that have been used to reach teenagers and educate them. Few have moved on radically from the rhetoric of the 'just say no' tactics, where education was based on fear rather than knowledge. Indeed, there is evidence that these warnings may actually stimulate drug experimentation. And there have been fewer still campaigns still aimed solely at heroin.

Today's youth knows that one puff on a joint doesn't lead inexorably to a full-blown heroin addiction, so drug-education messages need to accept that reality and ensure that messages are credible if kids are to listen to them in the first place. This means that, if the war against heroin is not winnable in absolute terms, then at least it will claim fewer casualties.

GLOSSARY

Agonist – A compound that will bind to a receptor and create a pharmacological response.

Analgesic – A drug that reduces pain. Analgesics act on the brain; opium derivatives such as morphine are powerful, but easily produce addiction. Non-narcotic analgesics, of which paracetamol and anti-inflammatories (such as aspirin) are the most common, act peripherally by preventing the formation of pain-producing substances, and are effective for headaches and minor pains.

Antagonist – A compound that will bind to a receptor to form a complex that does not give any response.

Codeine – Found in opium, but this mild to moderate painkiller is usually synthesized from morphine in medical products. Known on the streets as T-Three, cough syrup and schoolboy.

Drug – Any chemical substance that alters the physiological state of a living organism. Drugs are widely used in medicine for the prevention, diagnosis and treatment of diseases; they include analgesics, anaesthetics, antihistamines and anticoagulants.

Endomorphin – Two endogenous peptides that function as mu-agonists.

Endorphins – A peptide that functions as a selective agonist for the mu-opioid receptors.

Heroin – Heroin, or diacetylmorphine, is a narcotic compound that is a synthetic derivative of morphine. The compound is easily absorbed by the brain, and is used as a sedative and powerful analgesic. Very addictive.

Morphine – Naturally occurring substance in the opium poppy. Called

M, morph and Miss Emma on the streets, it is a potent narcotic analgesic.

Narcotic – A drug that induces drowsiness, stupor or insensibility. Narcotics include the opioid and synthesized compounds with morphine-like properties. They are powerful analgesics, used in medicine.

Opiate – One of a group of drugs derived from opium, an extract of the poppy plant that depresses brain function (a narcotic action). Opiates include morphine and its synthetic derivatives, such as heroin and codeine.

Opioid – Any one of a group of substances that produces pharmacological and physiological effects similar to those of morphine. Opioids are not necessarily structurally similar to morphine, and include fentanyl and methadone.

Papaver – A widely distributed, summer-flowering annual somniferum plant: *Papaver somniferum*, of the poppy family, Papaveraceae. It is grown in hot, dry climates for the drug opium, which is extracted from its sap. The raw material is refined to produce heroin.

Partial agonist – A compound that possesses affinity for a receptor, but will produce only a small pharmacological response.

Semi-synthetic – A compound with some opioid receptor similarities, synthesized by modification of product extracted from opium and including heroin.

Synthetic opiate – A compound with some opioid receptor similarities but using no material extracted from opium. Includes methadone.

TIMELINE

c3400 BC: The opium poppy is cultivated in lower Mesopotamia by the Sumerians, who would later pass on their poppy culling art to the Assyrians

c1300 BC: Egyptians begin cultivation of poppies in Thebes, and the opium trade flourishes under Thutmose IV

c1100 BC: Opium harvested on Cyprus

c460 BC: Hippocrates recognizes opium's use as a narcotic and for treating diseases

330 BC: Persia and India are introduced to opium by Alexander the Great

300 BC: Arabs, Greeks and Romans begin to use opium as a sedative

AD 400: Arab traders introduce opium to China

1300–1500: Opium becomes taboo and disappears from Europe for 200 years

1500: Portuguese traders begin the practice of smoking opium

1527: Laudanum painkillers, which contained opium, introduced to Europe

1606: Elizabeth I orders ships to transport Indian opium back to England

1680: Thomas Sydenham combines opium, sherry and herbs to produce Sydenham's Laudanum, which becomes a popular remedy for various ailments

1689: Tobacco is mixed with opium in East Indies opium dens

1700: Indian opium exported to China and Southeast Asia by the Dutch, who introduce the practice of smoking opium with a tobacco pipe

1729: Chinese emperor Yung Cheng prohibits opium smoking

1750: The British East India Company (BEIC) takes control of the Indian opium growing districts of Bihar and Bengal; Britain dominates the trade in opium between Calcutta and China

1767: The BEIC imports 2,000 chests of opium to China, most for medicinal use

1780: British traders establish an opium depot at Macao

1793: Indian poppy growers are only allowed to sell opium to the BEIC, which gains total monopoly over its trade

1796: China bans the import of opium, but illegal trade continues

1799: Opium poppy cultivation in China is banned

1803: Friedrich Sertürner discovers morphine, the active ingredient of opium, after dissolving it in acid and neutralizing it with ammonia

1804: Opium trading resumes at Canton, despite 1799 edict

1805: American smuggler Charles Cabot attempts to smuggle opium into China

1812-16: Opium smuggling becomes big business with trade between Turkey and Canton

1819: Writer John Keats and other literary figures, such as Byron and Coleridge, indulge in recreational use of opium

1821: Thomas De Quincey publishes *Confessions Of An English Opium Eater*

1827: The German pharmaceutical company, E Merck & Co, starts to manufacture morphine in commercial quantities

1832: Codeine extracted from opium

1839: The start of the first Opium War between Britain and China

1841: Britain defeats China, which cedes Hong Kong

1843: Dr Alexander Wood uses syringe to administer morphine

1852: British introduce Indian opium to Burma

1856: Second Opium War with China

1874: English researcher CR Alder Wright first synthesizes heroin; smoking
   opium banned in San Francisco

1878: Opium Act passed in Britain, which restricts the sale of opium to
   registered Chinese opium smokers

1890: US Congress imposes a tax on opium and morphine

1895: Working with morphine at the German company Bayer, Heinrich
   Dreser produces diacetylmorphine (heroin) and Bayer begins
   commercial production

1905: US bans opium

1906: Britain and China move to restrict the Sino-Indian opium trade;
   the US Pure Food and Drug Act requires medicines to label contents

1909: International Opium Commission in Shanghai

1910: Britain dismantles the opium trade between India and China

1914: Harrison Narcotics Act in USA, which requires pharmacists and
   doctors who prescribe heroin and other narcotics to register and
   pay tax

1923: US Treasury Department's Narcotics Division bans all narcotic
   sales, leading addicts to turn to illegal sources

1945: Burma gains independence, and opium cultivation and trade
   flourishes

1948: Corsican gangsters begin their illegal assault on the US market
   with heroin refined from Turkish opium in Marseille labs

1950s: US foreign policy aimed at containing the spread of communism
   in Asia (by financing and arming drug warlords in the 'Golden Triangle'
   – Myanmar, Laos, and Thailand) unwittingly increases production and
   flow of heroin

1962: Burma outlaws opium

1965-70: The number of heroin addicts in the USA estimated at around 750,000

1970: Controlled Substances Act passed in USA, divides drugs into groups and establishes penalties; the USA creates the Drug Enforcement Administration (DEA)

Mid-1970s: A new source of raw opium found in Mexico's Sierra Madre, which introduces 'Mexican mud' to US cities

1978: Opium fields in Mexico are sprayed with Agent Orange in a massive joint anti-drug initiative by the US and Mexican governments; drug smugglers turn to new supplies of opium from the 'Golden Crescent' – Iran, Afghanistan, Pakistan

1988: Opium production increases in Burma under the State Law and Order Restoration Council junta

1992: Colombia begins shipping high-grade heroin to the USA

1993: The Thai army and US DEA cooperate on destroying opium fields in the Golden Triangle

1995: The Golden Triangle becomes the world's biggest opium producer, with annual yields of 2,500 tonnes

1996-2002: Heroin trafficking continues to be problem with involvement of Chinese, Nigerian, Mexican and Colombian crime organizations

JUNKIE SLANG

AIP - heroin from Afghanistan, Iran and Pakistan

Atom bomb - heroin mixed with marijuana

Back to back - smoking crack after injecting heroin

Bad bundle - low-quality heroin

Bag - pack of heroin

Ball - Mexican black-tar heroin

Balloon - heroin dealer or balloon containing heroin

Belushi - cocaine and heroin

Bindle - small pack of heroin

Blank - non-narcotic powder passed off as heroin

Bomb - very potent heroin

Channel swimmer - someone who injects

Chasing the dragon - crack mixed with heroin, smoking heroin

Chase the tiger - to smoke heroin

China cat - very pure heroin

Chipper - occasional user

Chocolate chip cookies - MDMA mixed with heroin or methadone

Chocolate rock - crack smoked with heroin

Chucks - hunger following withdrawal

Cigarette paper - packet of heroin

Cook - to mix heroin with water; heating to prepare for injection

Cook down - to liquefy heroin in preparation for inhaling it

Cotton brothers - heroin, cocaine, and morphine

Crap - low-quality heroin

Criss-crossing - snorting up lines of cocaine and heroin simultaneously

Crop - low-quality heroin

Deck - between 1g and 15g (½oz) of heroin

Dime's worth - amount of heroin that would cause death

Dinosaurs - old users or addicts

Dragon rock - mixture of heroin and crack

Dust - to add heroin to marijuana

Dynamite - cocaine mixed with heroin

Eightball - crack mixed with heroin

Five way - snorting heroin, cocaine, methamphetamine, and crushed
    flunitrazepam pills, and drinking booze

Flamethrowers - cigarettes laced with heroin and cocaine

Flea powder - low-purity heroin

Foil - baking foil used to cook up and smoke heroin

Frisco special - heroin, cocaine and LSD

Frisco speedball - heroin, cocaine and a small amount of LSD

Garbage - inferior heroin

Get-off houses - places where users can buy and inject

Give wings - inject someone or teach them how to inject

Glass - hypodermic needle

Goofball - heroin mixed with cocaine

Gravy - to inject heroin

H&C - heroin and cocaine

H-bomb - heroin mixed with ecstasy

Half load - 15 bags of heroin

Half piece - 14g (½oz) of heroin

Homicide - heroin cut with scopolamine or strychnine

Hong yen - heroin in pill form

Horning – to inhale

Hot heroin – poisoned heroin

Hype – addict

Jolly pop – casual user

Jones – addiction

Karachi – heroin, phenobarbital, and methaqualone

LBJ – heroin, LSD, PCP

Lemonade – poor-quality heroin

Load – 25 bags of heroin

Meth speedball – methamphetamine mixed with heroin

Moonrock – heroin mixed with crack

Mortal combat – very pure heroin

Murder one – heroin and cocaine

New jack swing – heroin and morphine

Nod – using heroin

One-on-one house – place to buy heroin and cocaine

One-plus-one sales – selling heroin and cocaine together

P dope – 20-30 per cent pure heroin

Paper – a small dose of heroin

Paper boy – dealer

Polo – mix of heroin and motion sickness drug

Primos – cigarette laced with cocaine and heroin

Ragweed – poor-quality heroin

Red rock opium – heroin, barbital, strychnine, and caffeine

Red rum – another name for heroin, barbital, strychnine, and caffeine

Rider – 5kg (11lb) of free heroin on top of a 100kg (220lb) shipment of cocaine

This Is **HEROIN**

Sandwich – heroin between two layers of cocaine

Scramble – heroin cut with other drugs or non-narcotics

Serial speedballing – doing cocaine, cough syrup and heroin continuously over a couple of days

Shooting up – injecting

Smoking gun – heroin and cocaine

Sniffer bag – £3.45 ($5) bag of heroin intended for snorting

Snowball – cocaine and heroin

Speedball – cocaine mixed with heroin; crack with heroin smoked together; methylphenidate mixed with heroin

Speedballing – shooting up or smoking cocaine and heroin

Spike – heroin cut with scopolamine or strychnine; to inject; needle

Spoon – 1.75g (¹⁄₁₆oz) heroin; used to prepare heroin

Tar – crack and heroin smoked together

Taste – small sample of drug

Tecatos – Hispanic addict

Twists – small bags of heroin

Whack – heroin and PCP

Whiz bang – heroin and cocaine

Wicked – very pure heroin

Z – 28g (1oz) heroin